Crossing the Sands of Time

An Examination of the History and Legends of the Great Uighur Empire

---

Jack E. Churchward

Crossing the Sands of Time: An Examination of the History and Legends of the Great Uighur Empire

ISBN 978-1-7330566-0-1

Dedication

This work is dedicated to all peoples maintaining a peaceful struggle to preserve their cultural and linguistic identity in the face of state-sponsored attempts to erase their language, culture, and traditions.

Ilham Tohti's efforts to unite the citizens of the Peoples Republic of China exemplify the deeds of a great man. Knowing his words and actions to create an understanding of the peaceful Uyghur culture would cause his imprisonment, he continued to speak out against the harsh policies inflicted on his people. After receiving a life sentence for 'Separatist' crimes, he wrote these words:

> After seeing the judgment against me, contrary to what people may think, I now think I have a more important duty to bear.
>
> Even though I have departed, I still live in anticipation of the sun and the future. I am convinced that China will become better, and that the constitutional rights of the Uighur people will, one day, be honored.
>
> Peace is a heavenly gift to the Uighur and Han people. Only peace and good will can create a common interest.

Acknowledgements

For their assistance in providing data and advice, I wish to acknowledge the assistance of the following:
Dr. Dolkun Kamberi
Dr. Kahar Baret
Yannis Deliyannis

For permission to include his paper entitled, "Is Eastern Turkestan a Chinese Territory?", many thanks to Erkin Alptekin.

I wish to also acknowledge the assistance of the following individuals who reviewed and provided feedback:
Bruce Fenton
Carl Feagans
Uyghur scholar (unnamed for protection)

For permission to include portions of the *Books of The Golden Age* as an appendix, Richard Buhler of Brotherhood of Life Publishing.

Map Windows software used to create maps

Table of Contents

Illustrations

Illustrations contained in the Appendices have not been included.

Foreword

I was contacted by Jack Churchward in 1995 requesting information on the Uyghur people for the campaign against the Chinese government propaganda theme park in Florida. After he received a few copies of the Eastern Turkestan Information Bulletin of the Eastern Turkestan Union in Europe, he placed these online and we continued our correspondence, eventually placing all the ETIB issues and Common Voice, the publication of the Allied Committee for the Peoples of Eastern Turkestan, Inner Mongolia, and Tibet on the internet.

Jack continued to aid the Uyghur cause by building internet resources to discuss the deteriorating human rights situation in the People's Republic of China and organizing responses to the falsification of the history of the Uyghur, Mongol, and Tibetan peoples. He also supported the formation of the Uyghur American Association and was elected to their Board of Directors.

Through our correspondence and personal interactions at various meetings and conferences, I have found Jack to be a sincere advocate for human rights and this book is a continuation of his efforts to dispel the propaganda and false information about the Uyghur people.

For Freedom,
Erkin Alptekin
Former President of Unrepresented Nations and Peoples Organization (UNPO)
First President of World Uyghur Congress (WUC)

Preface

My initial research into Uyghur history was prompted by my involvement in political activism at the Florida Splendid China theme park in Kissimmee, Florida (12/19/1993 - 12/31/2003.) During this period, I interacted with many Tibetan, Mongolian, Chinese and Uyghur people and read as much of their histories as I could find. [see http://caccp.freedomsherald.org]

After the closing of the theme park, I spoke with the gentleman responsible for the Uyghur language version of the 1931 *Lost Continent of Mu* written by my great-grandfather. He asked me what I knew about the Great Uighur Empire. I proceeded to relate what I had learned from my research in countering the theme park's propaganda. He stopped me and said, "No, the one your great-grandfather wrote about in his books," Of course, I was intrigued and this encounter was one reason that I started my research into the life and writings of my great-grandfather, James Churchward.

One point I learned from my studies was a complete history of Inner Asia would be impossible to compose without including the Uyghur people. Although hardly a household word in the US, their contributions to Asian history and culture span many centuries. Their achievements in agriculture, literature and music created a standalone civilization; unique from the other peoples of Central and Inner Asia.

Given my unique position as a continuing student of history, my activities in opposition to propaganda, and my last name, I feel an obligation to set the record straight. What I found in my research of Asian history differed greatly from what I read in my great-grandfather's works. My self-imposed duty is to provide an accurate account to correct the record, especially in light of the current campaign of cultural genocide waged upon the 'minority' people of the Peoples Republic of China. The truth must be told.

My only agenda is to promote the true history of my friends. I believe in the unfettered life, liberty and happiness for

Uyghur language, culture, and people against the pressures of a dictatorial government. Like the Tibetans and Mongolians, also under pressure to extinguish their cultural identity, the homeland of the Uyghur people serves as the backdrop for fantastic tales and it is only fair that an accurate historical account be available.

The first portion of this work deals with the historical Great Uighur Khaganate that lasted from 744 to 840 C.E. and a subsequent history of the Uyghur people. Following portions examine other theories and writings evoking the name.

Part 1: Historical Uighur Empire

Chapter 1: Early Inner Asia

To differentiate fact from fiction, the first part of this work provides the context for the examination of the history of the Great Uighur Empire. Myths, legends, and various other recounting of seemingly mysterious and bizarre happenings, customs, and peoples have clouded the common perception of Inner Asia. Late 19th and early 20th century accounts relied on the personal experiences of a few explorers; their reports colored by the fantastic tales heard along their route. Unfamiliar surroundings and a need to maintain their benefactors' interest in their discoveries also contributed to some misunderstandings. Additionally, emperors, kings, khans and other heads of state instigate a further departure from the truth with their propaganda. Inner Asia was a mysterious place once, a vast track of land with the highest mountains, deepest lakes and the coldest deserts. Building on the mysteries of this harsh environment, some believed it to be the birthplace of the human race, the real Garden of Eden. Of course, James Churchward wrote of his Great Uighur Empire, the primary colony of the sunken continent of Mu dating back tens of thousands of years, covering most of Asia and Europe. What does the evidence say about all these things? What does the written and archaeological history reveal about the truth? The following pages provide some answers to these questions.

Inner Asia encompasses a vast stretch of land not including eastern and southeastern Asia, India, Japan or the Koreas, but does include the Central Asian nations (Uzbekistan, Kyrgyzstan, Kazakhstan, Turkmenistan, Tajikistan,) Tibet, Siberia, East Turkestan (aka Xinjiang,) Manchuria, and Mongolia (north and south.) For the purpose of this discussion, Inner Asia's southern boundary loosely begins just north of where agricultural societies established themselves (as opposed to pastoral societies) and continues north to the frozen Arctic. This is a broad generalization; descriptions in other books fill entire long chapters. The actual boundary shifted over the centuries as climates changed and modernity changed lifestyles.

The Eurasian Steppe penetrates the core of Inner Asia, stretching thousands of miles from Hungary through Ukraine,

Russia, Turkestan, Mongolia and on to Manchuria. A nearly continuous swath of grasslands lying dormant from the cold in winter and parched during the summer heat, it is bordered by forests, mountains and deserts. The Steppe became the hominid highway in both directions, permitting access to new lands, food sources and the freedom to begin life anew. European history records the encroachment of Huns, Avars, Vandals, and Mongols. In the other direction, there came the Yamnaya, Andronovo, Afanasevo, and Tokharians. These are only the migrations history and archaeology have recorded in the past few thousand years; evidence of Neanderthal occupation dates back at least 125,000 years in southern Siberia. The Steppe's grasslands have facilitated hominid migrations for at least that long.

At one time, scientific circles heralded Asia as the location where modern humans first arose. Alexander Graham Bells' father-in-law, Gardiner G. Hubbard, in his address before the Geographic Society on March 14, 1890 began with these words on the location of the 'Garden of Eden.'

> ASIA, the birthplace of man, the mother of nations, is our theme to-night. Here are found the two great races of the world, the Mongolian and Caucasian; here the great religions of the world had their origin, the Jews, the Buddhists, the Christians, and Mohammedans. Here is the Pamir, the "roof of the world" or the steps to heaven, the abode of the gods; the centre of primeval tradition, as well as of modern theory regarding the primitive history of man. Here the Paradise of Adam has been most frequently located. Here is the lake from which the four rivers of the Garden of Eden diverge to the four quarters of the earth.
> Science, Vol. 15, No. 371 (Mar. 14, 1890), pp. 170-175

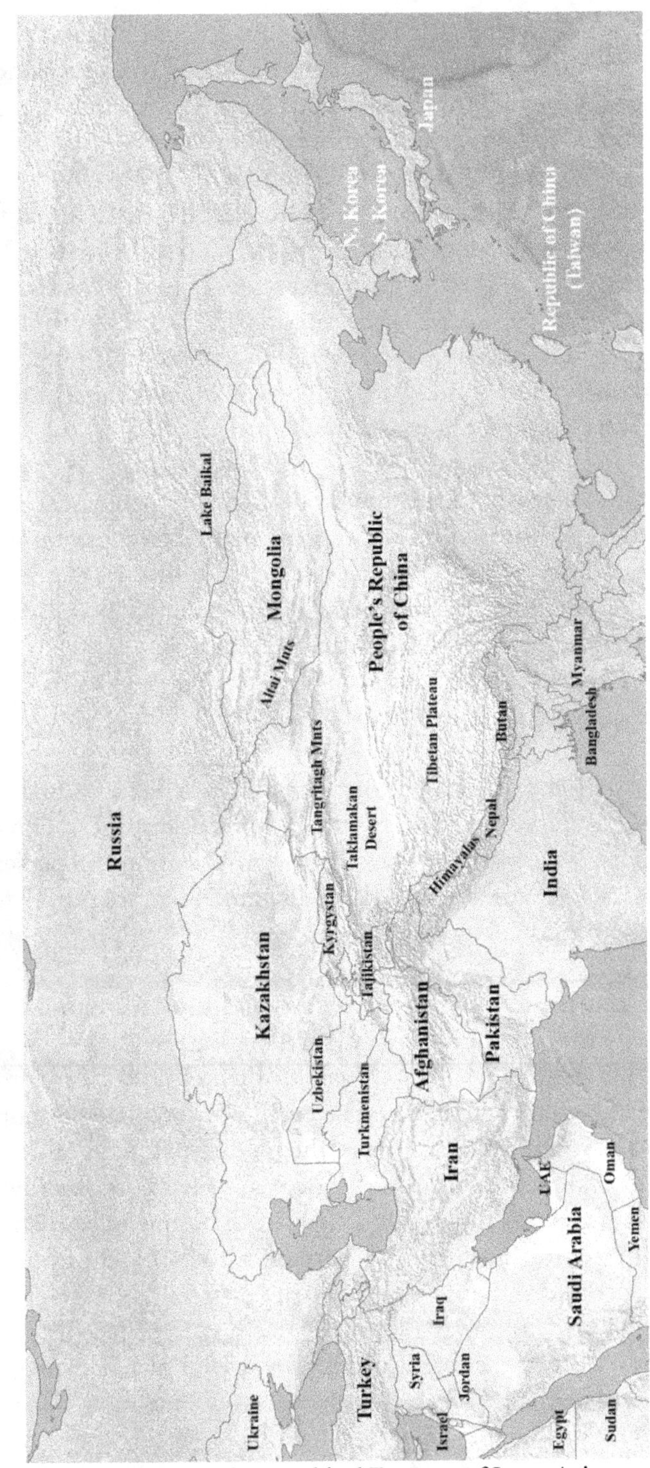

Figure 1: Geographical Features of Inner Asia

Ernst Haeckel (1834-1919) theorized sub-humans first arose in Lemuria, a sunken continent proposed to explain the distribution of lemur fossils around the Indian Ocean basin. He also used the now-sunken connection between Asia and Africa to account for the initial migration of humanity. In his theory, the missing link from Lemuria migrated and evolved into the humans of today in Asia. From there, they spread across the planet. The discovery of hominid remains in Java, now identified as Homo erectus, appeared to support this theory. Theosophy author W. Scott-Elliot in *The Lost Lemuria* (1904) points to Indian Ocean islanders and others as the "degraded remnants of the Third Root race" that inhabited Lemuria.

Alas, a greater understanding of Earth's geological processes has dismissed these theories. Plate tectonics accounted for the distribution of the fossil evidence without the need for a sunken continent and Lemuria disappeared from serious scientific literature soon thereafter. Without the Lemurians as our forebears, we must also reject the nonsense of portraying the Indian Ocean islanders as something less than human.

A better explanation for the early presence of hominids in Asia is the Eurasian Steppe and the indomitable spirit to explore and seek greener pastures. We still have those genes, to persevere, to adapt, to learn, to control our environment and the drive to advance our kind.

To make another point, history indicates a continual advancement of their cultures and civilizations, with no discontinuities suggesting an infusion of technology from a more advanced civilization. Ancient historical (non-religious) documents indicate a smooth transition from the picture painted in the archaeological record. Simply put, no evidence exists to show any of their civilizations radically changed after contact with a superior 'civilizing' empire. To suggest otherwise is to rob them of their rightful accomplishments and their true history. The next few paragraphs provide a bare outline of this history; enough to provide an historical context of the Great Uighur Khaganate / Empire within Inner Asia.

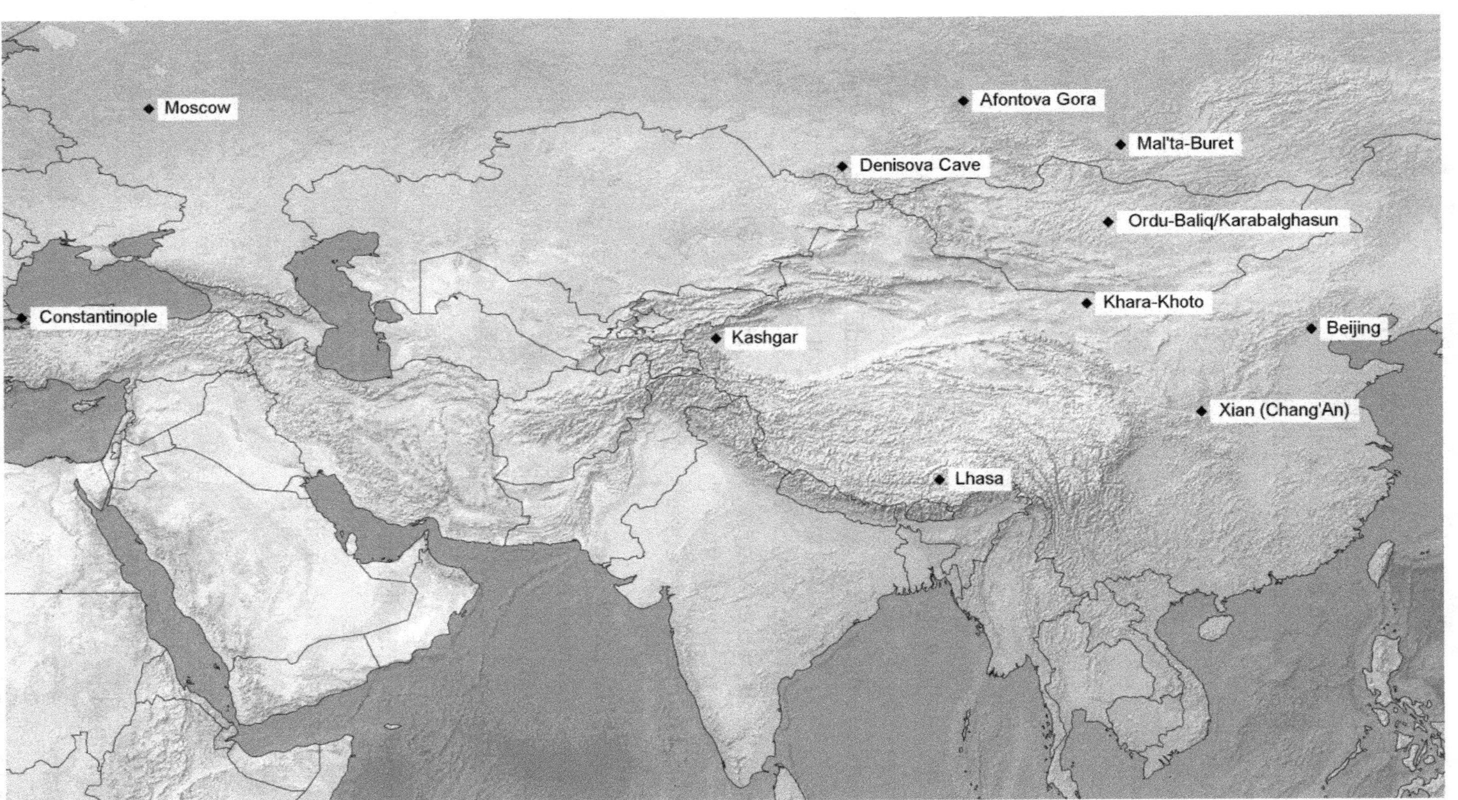

Figure 2: Locations of Interest

The Altai Mountains of southern Siberia are home to excellent examples of early hominid occupation in Inner Asia. The Denisova cave in the Bashelaksky Range contains evidence of hominid activity dating back 125,000 years BP. Some place habitation back 282,000 years BP; however, confirmation of that analysis is ongoing. Authorities named the cave after the 18th century human resident of the cave, Dionisij (Denis,) a Russian hermit.

Archaeologists discovered Levallois and Mousterian style stone tools generally associated with Neanderthal in an Upper Paleolithic layer from 46,000 BP. Evidence of their daily lives included decorations created from mammoth tusk, bone, animal teeth, mollusk shell fashioned into beads, pendants, and even fragments of a drilled and polished bracelet. At a layer dated 50,000 years BP, the earliest known needle made of bird bone was recently unearthed. These finds paint a different picture than would have been evoked one hundred or more years ago. Once considered ugly brutes, we now know Neanderthal possessed qualities we recognize today as human in spite of their physical differences from Homo sapiens sapiens.

The Denisova cave also revealed an extinct species or sub-species of human from DNA analysis of remains dating 30-50,000 years BP. They became the Denisovans. It would be pure speculation to associate the two peoples as living together simultaneously in this location; however, the existence of Neanderthal and Denisovan DNA in the human gene pool does allow such a possibility. Finds of a more recent age indicate modern humans also shared the shelter of the Denisova cave, the one known habitation shared by all three hominids.

Far from being a singular occurrence, the excavations at the Okladnikov Cave, about 30 miles away from the Denisova Cave, also records Neanderthal activity. Dated to 43,000 years ago, the discoveries from this site expanded the range of Neanderthal habitation in Asia when first excavated in 1984.

Modern humans also inhabited the Inner Asian grasslands and beyond in ancient times. Evidence of human habitation in

Japan reaches back 47,000 years BP. In our area of discussion, dating to 24,000 to 15,000 BP, the humans of the Mal'ta-Buret' culture lived a sedentary life west of Lake Baikal along the Angara River. To brave the freezing Siberian climate, they constructed pit-houses up to 14 feet in diameter. Using large mammoth bones and reindeer antlers, they propped up a covering made of animal skins and sod over an excavated circular depression. In some instances, the shelter also contained a low wall of stones around the pit at ground level to provide further support. Each of the family-sized dwellings had a central hearth lined with stones. They had no large settlements, just small groups braving the environment. Hunter-gatherers, they manufactured stone tools and implements of bone used to hunt small and large game.

The archaeological excavations by M.M. Gerasimov in the late 1920s yielded a curious distribution of items within the dwellings; to the right of the fire-place were found hunting weapons and carved bird figurines; the left side were found knives, scrapers, awls, necklaces, pendants, and carved statues of women. He postulated the partition as males on the right and females on the left side; equating the different sides with the roles of males as hunters and the women as homemakers (or family managers.) Of course, some researchers are challenging this theory.

Like so many other ancient cultures, the people identified as the Mal'ta-Buret' culture no longer survive as a distinct people. However, according to the experts, they passed along a significant genetic contribution to Siberians, Native Americans, and the Yamna. The Yamnaya (3,500-2,500 BCE), a Bronze Age people from Western Europe, are believed to have formed the homeland of the Indo-European language and are closely related to other European and Central Asian peoples.

Another Siberian archaeological complex from the Upper Paleolithic and hundreds of miles further north and west, Afontova Gora, shows cultural and genetic links with Mal'ta-Buret'. Dating to 20,000 to 18,000 years BP, they lived on the banks of the Yenisei River, hunting mammoth and other game with stone implements. They also created art, such as beads and pendants and fashioned needles, drills and other implements from the bones of their quarry.

Figure 3: Engraving of a mammoth on a slab of mammoth ivory, from the Upper Paleolithic (24,000 – 15,000 years BP) Mal'ta deposits at Lake Baikal, Siberia

A people that experts say are genetically indistinguishable from the Yamna people, known as the Afanasevo, were another early Bronze Age people inhabiting the Altai Mountains in southern Siberia. Their culture thrived from 3,300 to 2,500 BC and no longer relied on the hunt to feed their people. They raised cattle, sheep and horses; but had not yet mastered agriculture. Their craftsmen still made tools of stone and bone, but they added metallurgy to their repertoire. Another advancement attributed to the Afanasevo is the domestication of the horse. Their artistic representations of wheeled vehicles and carved pieces of antler functioning as a primitive form of halter or bridle provide support for this theory.

Subsequently, the nomadic Andronovo culture (2,000 – 900 BCE) appeared across the Eurasian Steppe. Related to other Indo-European groups, they built settlements, but also retained their mobility. Their livestock included camels, cattle, goats, horses and sheep. They used horses for riding and pulling their wheeled vehicles and engaged in agriculture. Evidence of the mining of copper and workshops dating to 1,400 BCE indicate their capabilities in metallurgy. They buried their dead under kurgans (tumuli) in rock or timber lined chambers accompanied by their livestock, weapons, ceramics, ornaments and their wheeled vehicles. Much research has shown the Andronovo to be an Indo-Iranian (Aryan) people with Caucasian features; however, some dispute the language affiliation. On the other hand, DNA testing of a sample of Andronovo burials from 1400 to 1000 BCE indicated

78% were Caucasian and the remainder 'Mongoloid'; the majority was blue-eyed and light haired.

These are a few examples of a very long list of known hominid habitation sites in Inner Asia spanning tens of thousands of years. This is the evidence gleamed from the archaeological record. A list of the myriad cultures and peoples starting, flowering and then withering into obscurity will probably never be complete; however, the record is clear. Inner Asia and the Eurasian Steppe facilitated human migrations and supported a human population for millennia, satisfying the wanderlust of those brave and strong enough to venture into unknown lands to stake out a brighter future. The Uyghur people are descendants of the Inner Asian mixing bowl; their culture and life-experience forged through tens of thousands of years interacting with harsh environments, changing life-styles and different peoples.

Archaeological endeavors continue to add to our understanding of Inner Asia history. The written records kept by ancient peoples add color to the otherwise black and white facts pulled from the ground. The ancient records reveal the writer's thoughts and impressions into his/her life and surroundings and occasionally the uncensored truth leaks out. The following paragraphs explore the history of the people who would one day form the Great Uighur Empire and how they earned the right to be the 'Great' Uighur Empire. First, we start with the Xiongnu, one of the first nomadic peoples mentioned in ancient Chinese records.

The Xiongnu (Hsiung Nu)

During the late Warring States period (475 BCE – 221 BCE) in Chinese history, the three northern players were required to address the encroachment of their northern nomadic neighbors. This was in addition to their conflicts with the other early Chinese states. To prevent the raiding and pillaging, they built and manned border walls consisting of rammed earth and gravel between board frames. The Qin (Ch'in) started their northern barrier in 324 BCE and completed work about 270 BCE. The Zhao (Chao) completed their defensive structure around 300 BCE, and a decade later the Yan (Yen) completed their portion. The creation of these defensive structures is the first mention in written Chinese records directly related to the Xiongnu. Although earlier records speak of the northern nomads, these accounts can be directly attributable to the Xiongnu, or actually the defense against them. After the Qin subdued the other six states and created a unified state (221 BCE,) Qin Shi Huangdi (Ch'in Shih Huang-ti,) (259 – 210 BCE,) the self-described First Emperor of China, continued on the offense and defense. Pushing the nomadic Xiongnu and Donghu (Tung-hu) further north to expand his territory, the Qin Emperor also worked to consolidate the walls constructed a hundred years earlier, forming the basis for the Great Wall of China. The form of the wall most familiar to people today were constructed in the 14th century during the Ming Dynasty and apply better construction techniques, using bricks and stones to form the barrier. The Qin capital city became Xianyang near Xian (known as Chang'an before the Ming dynasty) in Shaanxi (Shensi) province.

The Xiongnu were nomadic, ever moving with their livestock in search of fresh pastures and fresh sources of water. Along with flocks of sheep, the Xiongnu also raised and maintained herds of horses, cattle and camels. According to ancient Chinese records, they ate only meat and slept on furs in their felt tents. The records describe them as short and stocky with large round heads and broad faces. Modern archaeological evidence cited by Chinese historian Lin Gan indicates the Xiongnu looked Caucasian. They dressed in a loose robe to the calf with trousers, leather shoes, short fur cape on the shoulders and a fur cap to top off their wardrobe. Nomadic peoples maintained the same wardrobe across the Steppe for centuries. Another similarity among the Steppe nomads was the practice of Tengrism. Their belief system had elements of shamanism, animism, and ancestor worship. The core belief was in Tengri, the Heavenly Father; the celestial god who created all things and watched from heaven. In their pastoral lifestyle, the Xiongnu lived in harmony with the grasslands. Unfortunately, their neighbors were not able to live in harmony with the Xiongnu.

Facing the unified Chinese Empire to the south, the nomads to east called the Donghu, the nomads to the west called the Yuezhi (Yueh-chih,) the Dingling (Ting-ling) and other tribes to the north, the Xiongnu Tengriqut (shan-yu) Touman (Tumen) started the consolidation of the Xiongnu. Around 209 BCE,

Touman sent his eldest son, Batur (Motun) to the Yuezhi as a hostage to create a peace between the two peoples. Obviously, Batur was not the favored son since shortly thereafter Touman launched an attack on the Yuezhi. Before the Yuezhi effected punishment for his father's treachery, Batur stole a fast horse and escaped. Upon his return and for his bravery, his father rewarded him with 10,000 mounted bowmen. Plotting revenge for his betrayal, Batur trained his bowmen to shoot without hesitation at the target he first shot with a special whistling arrow; death was immediate for those bowmen who hesitated. He tested his troops by shooting at his favorite horse and then his favorite wife. When none balked after he shot his father's favorite horse, he then shot at his father, Touman. Next, he eliminated those members of his family who had plotted against him and uncooperative officials. Batur became Tengriqut Batur, leader of the first great nomadic empire of the steppes, the Xiongnu. Batur did not rest on his laurels, but set upon his eastern neighbors, the Donghu. Killing their leader and capturing much livestock and prisoners, he then turned his attention to his western and northern neighbors. Heading south, Tengriqut Batur recaptured the Xiongnu lands the Qin had taken earlier.

Tengriqut Batur's expansion of Xiongnu control signaled a new era in the relationship with the Chinese state to the south. After the collapse of the Qin, the Han dynasty (206 BCE-220 CE) assumed the reins of power in China and quickly became at odds with the Xiongnu. The Xiongnu continued to gobble up territory and raid cities, towns and villages. In 200 BCE, Han Emperor Gaozu (Kao-Tsu) (256-195 BCE) set out from his capital Chang'an, attempting a military solution to the problem. His attempt to lead and confront the Xiongnu with an army of 300,000 did not end well. The Xiongnu surrounded them with as many horsemen and the Emperor barely escaped. Emperor Gaozu decided on a different approach to alleviate the hassle and instability caused by his northern neighbors – tribute.

Beginning in 198 BCE, the Xiongnu and Han entered into the first Heqin (Ho-ch'in) peace alliance. In return for the Xiongnu's implied promise to stop hostilities, Tengriqut Batur received Gaozu's eldest daughter as a bride. The Xiongnu also received tribute several times a year; the Han would send various kinds of gifts, including fixed amounts of silks, food and wine. Additionally, the Han recognized the Xiongnu as a brother state, equal in status to the Han.

The shaky Heqin relationship lasted over seventy years before the Han had enough. They had enough of the raids and the ever-increasing gifts. In 134 BCE, the young Han Emperor Wu (156 – 87 BCE,) at the suggestion of a border merchant, conspired to eliminate the problem all together. The merchant befriended the Tengriqut and planned to set a trap for him and his army that ultimately failed. Full-scale war did not start for another five years and even then, it was not until 127 BCE a major offensive proved detrimental to the Xiongnu cause.

The Xiongnu also interacted with their other neighbors, including the Yuezhi, Batur Tengriqut's former captors. Around 174 BCE, Batur Tengriqut 's son Jizhu (Chi-chu, aka Laoshang) in accordance with nomadic traditions killed the Yuezhi king, made a drinking cup from his skull and drove the Yuezhi from what today is Gansu (Kansu.) The migration of those renamed the Great Yuezhi travelled to the Ili Valley where they displaced a Scythian people, Indo-European descendants of the Andronovo. The Xiongnu co-opted the assistance of the Wusun and in 134 BCE again attacked the Great Yuezhi, forcing them to flee south-west.

The Xiongnu interacted with their eastern neighbors, the Donghu. These were two tribes named Wuhuan and Xianbei (Hsein-pei,) that had migrated north into territory once known as Manchuria. They remained under the control of the Xiongnu and offered tribute as well. Annually, the Xiongnu demanded sable skins, oxen, sheep and horses from the Wuhuan and when their tribute did not arrive, inevitably, the Xiongnu captured and enslaved their women and children. Eventually, the remaining Wuhuan migrated south and assimilated into the Chinese people. The Xianbei, on the other hand, remained nomadic and allied with the Xiongnu.

The northern neighbors, the Dingling people, maintained their nomadic ways as part of the Xiongnu and revolted in 71 BCE. They also joined the Wusun and Chinese to attack the Xiongnu in actions between 63 and 60 BCE. In 51 BCE, the

Tengriqut Zhizhi subjugated the Dingling, bringing them back into the fold. Joining with the Xianbei in 85 CE, the Dingling helped end Xiongnu dominance. The Dingling disappeared into the Xianbei and remnants of the Xiongnu, however Chinese sources place them as related to the Tiele (T'ieh-lê.) There will be more said of the Tiele.

After the collapse of the Heqin relationship, the Han went on the offensive and reconquered the borderlands. By building alliances with the Xiongnu's vassal states, they were able to erode Xiongnu control, eventually capturing and holding the western lands around the Tarim Basin (East Turkestan / 'Xinjiang') and as far west as the Fergana Valley (in Uzbekistan.) Han dynasty China gained control of the western regions of the Xiongnu Empire in 60 BCE. The weakened nomad empire, due to political pressures, eventually split into the North and South factions and the Southern Xiongnu became allies of the Chinese. The northern Xiongnu were finally 'crushed and subjugated' by the Xianbei in 155 CE. The southern Xiongnu resettled behind the Great Wall and assimilated into the Chinese people. In 304 CE, their descendants created the Former Zhao dynasty lasting twenty-five years.

The Xiongnu were the first great nomadic power based in the Mongolian Steppe and at times, wielded enormous political and military power. Their presence in the grasslands and beyond had a profound effect on Inner Asia. The northern 'barbarians' created a need for the Great Wall of China, improved foreign statecraft, and advancements in military technology and tactics.

The Xianbei confederacy gained power in Inner Asia when Xiongnu power waned. Lasting from about 93 to 243 CE, they were a nomadic empire and, as the Xiongnu before them, interacted with their southern neighbors, the Chinese. As with the other 'barbarians,' many were introduced to Chinese customs, assimilated and ultimately established themselves as a political presence behind the Great Wall.

After most of the Xianbei migrated south, the Rouran (Juan Juan) ascended as the new nomadic power and established their own confederacy from 330-552 CE. The Gok-Turk were members of this confederacy. As loyal vassals of the Rouran, the

Gok-Turk leader, Bumin, alerted the Rouran of an impending attack from the Tiele and saved the Rouran from an ignoble defeat. The Tiele, a neighboring nomadic confederation, contained nine Turkic tribes, the Uighur being one of them. When A-na-kui, the last Rouran leader, rebuffed Bumin's request for royal bride, the Gok-Turks revolted with the Xianbei of the Western Wei and formed a new khaganate.

First Gok-Turk Khaganate

What we know of the Xiongnu, Xianbei, and Rouran mostly comes from Chinese records. In contrast, Byzantine and Persian as well as Chinese records describe the people and interactions of the Gok-Turk Khaganate. Their influence was not just limited to Inner Asia but stretched far to the West as well.

The Gok-Turks also created their own records, monuments in stone lauding the great accomplishments of their Khagans. One such record is contained in a memorial complex in the Orkhon Valley of today's Mongolia about twenty-five miles south of their nomadic capital. Carved in Old Turkic runes as well as in Chinese and Sogdian script and originally mounted on top of carved stone turtles, the great steles extol the words and deeds of Bilge Khagan and his brother Kol-Tegin of the second Gok-Turk Khaganate. Their words concerning the beginnings of the Gok-Turk Khaganate are as follows:

> When the blue sky above and the dark earth below were made, then were made between them both the sons of men. Over the sons of men set themselves [as rulers] my forbears Bumin kagan and Istaemi kagan, and having set themselves [as rulers] they governed and kept in order the Turkic peoples' kingdoms and polity. All [the peoples in] the four quarters of the world were foes to them; but they waged wars against them and overcame all the peoples in the four quarters of the world, made them keep the peace and bow their head and bend their knee.
> Orkhon Monument 1, East Side.

Members of the Ashina clan of the Gok-Turk formed the First Turkic Khaganate in 552 CE under the leadership of Bumin

Khagan. His sudden death a short time later brought his son, Muhan, to the leadership of the Eastern Gok-Turks with the title of Khagan and responsibility for Mongolia. Ishtemi, Bumin's brother, became the leader of the Western Gok-Turks with the title of yabghu and responsibility for the Western lands.

Although named the Gok-Turk Khaganate, many different peoples lived under their rule and not all of them were ethnically Turkic. While many of the khaganate followed the beliefs of their ancestors in Tengri, the Eternal Sky God, they also tolerated the observance of Buddhism, Manichaeism, and Nestorian Christianity.

The Western Gok-Turks interacted with the Persians under Khosrow I (496 – 579 CE,) entering into a military alliance and assisting them in conquering the Hephthalites (557-561 CE.) The Sasanian Emperor even married a daughter of the Turk ruler to cement their alliance. After the defeat of the Hephthalites, the friendly relationship deteriorated.

The first Gok-Turk delegation visited the Byzantine capital of Constantinople in 563 CE to discuss commercial matters during the reign of Justinian (482 – 565 CE.) Other topics of discussion could have been an alliance to rid them of their common enemy, the Persians. Western Gok-Turk and Byzantine delegations continued to meet in both capitals on a regular basis. Sogdians representing Ishtemi met with Byzantine Emperor Justin II (520 – 578 C) to rid themselves of Persian middlemen in the trading of Chinese silk.

After the death of the Eastern Gok-Turk Khagan Taspar, Ishtemi's son Tardu yabghu, now leader of the Western Gok-Turk bestowed on himself the title of Khagan in 581 CE and attacked the Eastern Gok-Turk. His attempt was unsuccessful but signaled an irreconcilable split in the Khaganate between East and West.

Eventually internal conflicts weakened the Eastern Gok-Turk and Chinese intrigue supported rival internal factions against their Khagan, Illig. In 630 CE, Illig was captured by the Chinese and lived as a prisoner for the next four years until his death. The

Tiele assisted in bringing the Eastern Gok-Turk Khaganate under Chinese control for the next fifty-two years (630-682 CE.)

Also in 630 CE, Tung yabghu, leader of the Western Gok-Turk Khaganate, died at the hands of another rebel Tiele tribe, the Karluks. The Western Gok-Turk Khaganate lasted another 27 years before it also collapsed. Tang Dynasty Emperor Gaozong (628 – 683 CE) claimed the title of Khagan of the Western Gok-Turks in 657 CE and exercised indirect control of the Silk Road from Persia (Iran) to Tang China.

Second Gok-Turk Khaganate

Distant relatives of Illig Khagan, Elterish and his brother Kapghan united the remnants of the Gok-Turk Empire and revolted against the Chinese Tang dynasty in 679 CE. In 682 CE, the second Gok-Turk Khaganate was established. The Toquz Oghuz, a confederacy of Tiele tribes, as well as peoples from across the first Gok-Turk Khaganate, submitted to the new Turkic rulers. After the death of Elterish (694 CE,) Kapghan (also known as Mocho) took over leadership and sought rapprochement with Chinese. They bestowed Kapghan with honorific titles for his aid in crushing the Qidans (Kitans) and conceded to his demands to repatriate the Turks who had settled in the Ordos region. Additionally, the Chinese gave a substantial supply of grain and thousands of pieces of farm implements. Unfortunately, internal conflicts kept the alliances of their subjects constantly changing until his enemies ambushed and killed him in 716 CE. Kapghan's son became the third Gok-Turk leader, Enel Khagan

After Kol Tegin (684 – 731 CE,) younger son of Elterish dispatched Enel and his other cousins, he placed his older brother Bilge (683 – 734 CE) on the throne. Both brothers had a markedly different relationship than previous leaders and worked in harmony together and with the Tang Chinese.

Bilge Khagan's words on the Orkhon Inscription relate the following:

> …to the end that the Turkic people should not perish but that it should [again] become a people, they raised up my father Elterish kagan and my mother Elbilga katun,

supporting them from the heights of Heaven. My father the kagan went forth with seventeen men. When they heard the tidings that he was going forth outside [China], they that were in the towns went out, and they that were on the mountains came down from them, and when they gathered together they were seventy men. As Heaven gave them strength, my father, the kagan's army was as wolves, and their foes as sheep. Making marches East and West, he gathered people and brought them together, and there came to be in all seven hundred men. When there had come to be seven hundred men he set the people in order in consonance with my forefathers' institutions, the people that had lost its realms and its kagan, the people that had become thralls and slave-women, the people whose Turkic institutions had been broken up, and he put heart into them. He now brought order into the Tölish peoples and the Tardush peoples, and gave them a yabgu and a shad. To the south the Chinese people was our foe, to the North Baz kagan and the people of the Tokuz [" Nine "] Oguz's were our foes; Kirghiz, kurikans, Otuz [" Thirty "] Tatars, Kitays and Tatabis-they were all hostile to us; (with) all these (had) my father the kagan (to fight ?). Forty-seven times he went campaigning, and fought in twenty fights. By the will of Heaven we took from them that had a kingdom their kingdom, and them that had a kagan we robbed of their kagan; he made the foes to keep the peace, and made them bow their head and bend their knee.

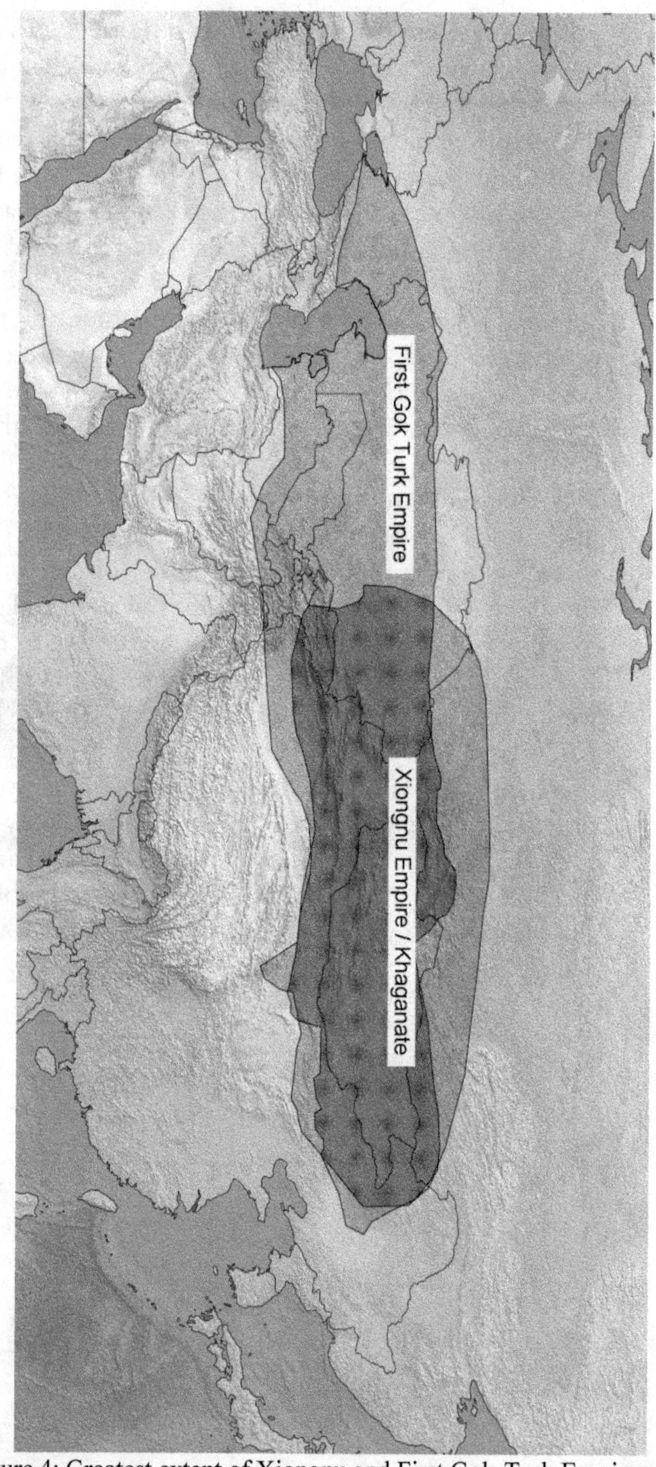

Figure 4: Greatest extent of Xiongnu and First Gok-Turk Empires

The death of Kol Tegin in 731 was a terrible blow to Bilge Khagan. The Tang Emperor Xuanzong (Hsuan-tsung) (685 – 762 CE) was so moved, he ordered a funeral stele erected in his honor and sent six famous painters to depict his greatest battles on the walls of a temple also built in his honor. The Emperor also consented to the marriage of Bilge Khagan to an imperial princess. Internal conflicts again arose and in 734 CE, a trusted member of his entourage poisoned Bilge Khagan. In the next decade, the Second Gok-Turk Khaganate began a rapid decline until the final Gok-Turk Khagan succumbed to a revolt by the Basmils, Karluks and Uighurs. In 745 CE, Emperor Xuanzong received the head of the last Gok-Turk Khagan, Ozmis Khagan.

Chapter 2: The Great Uighur Empire

> "... this country of barbarous customs, full of the fumes of blood, was changed into a land where the people live on vegetables; from a land of killing to a land where good deeds are fostered."
> Karabalghasun Inscription describing the Uighur Empire

According to Chinese sources, the nomadic Dingling people, once part of the Xiongnu Khaganate, were associated with the Tiele (aka Chile, Gaoche or Tele.) The ancestors of the Uighur were called Gui Gang in the distant past, even prior to the Xiongnu. According to Chinese historian Qian Boquan, the original pronunciation of Gui was 'Ugur' in ancient times. The Tiele were an Inner Asian confederation of Turkic tribes during the fourth and fifth centuries. During the Second Gok-Turk Khaganate, members of the Tiele, including the Uighur aligned themselves as the Toquz Oghuz (the Nine Oghuz.) The words of Bilge Khagan, son of the founder of the second Gok-Turk khaganate, on the Orkhon Inscriptions relate the following concerning the Toquz Oghuz:

> The Tokuz-Oguz people were my own people. As Heaven and Earth were in turmoil they rose against us. Within one year we fought five times...
> The Tokuz-Oguz's were my own people. Since Heaven and earth were in a tumult, and since envy have taken hold of their mind, they rose in rebellion. Within one year I fought four times...
> The Tokuz-Oguz people left their land, and went to China. (... from) China they came (back) to this land.

Only a few short years after craftsmen chiseled these words into stone to commemorate the Gok-Turk Khaganate established by Bumin Khagan almost two hundred years earlier, the Uighur rose to power. The tribes of the Toquz Oghuz confederation consisted of the Uighur, the Bokhu, the Khun, the Bayirku, and the Tongra. Chinese history relates the remaining four as the Ssu-Chieh, the Ch'i-pi, the A-pu-ssu, and the Ku-lun-wu-ku. The Uighur consisted of ten clans called the On Uighur (Ten Uighur) whose dominant clan was the Yaghlakar. Kol Bilge (Guli Peiluo,) the leader of the Yaghlakar clan, campaigned with his forces and their Basmil and Karluk neighbors to overcome Gok-Turk dominance. In their efforts, the Basmil captured the Gok-Turk capital and delivered the head of the last Gok-Turk Khagan to the Chinese Emperor in 745 CE, signaling the end of the second Gok-Turk Khaganate.

The Karluk and Uighur soon deposed the Basmil, beheaded their leader and dispersed their people. The Uighur leader and organizer of the coalition became the Khagan and the Karluk leader carried the title 'yabgu.' Kol Bilge, the first Khagan of the Great Uighur Empire took his throne name as Kutluk Kol Bilge Khagan (Glorious, Wise, Mighty Khagan.) He built his capital on top of the former Gok-Turk capital in the Orkhon Valley of today's Mongolia. He named it Ordu Baliq (known to the Mongols as Karabalghasun, the "Black City.") This new alliance did not last long and within the year, hostilities broke out between the Karluk and Uighur, ending in the westward migration of the Karluk.

To the new ruler, the Uighur carried forward the banner of the Gok-Turk Khaganate established by Bumin; they based their legitimacy on following the same traditions as their forefathers in the previous khaganates. One very important tradition was the special significance of sacred Mount Otuken. Each of the previous Turkic states built their capitals in the shadow of a Mount Otuken in the Orkhon Valley, a tradition that continued into the 13th century with the Mongol Empire. Another tradition inscribed on the Orkhon Inscription was "if thou stay on in the mountain forest of Otukan, thou shalt ever hold an everlasting kingdom."

Inner Asia had been in turmoil with political intrigue and outright warfare before and during the rise of the Uighur Empire. Tang dynasty China had reasserted their control over the Tarim Basin and beyond, struggling to keep back the invading Arabs and Tibetans. The threat of the invading armies became a great selling point for accepting China's protection for the non-Chinese inhabitants. According to the New Tang History (1060 CE,) with the collapse of the Gok-Turk Khaganate, the lands from the Altai Mountains to Lake Baikal and the Gobi Desert came under the

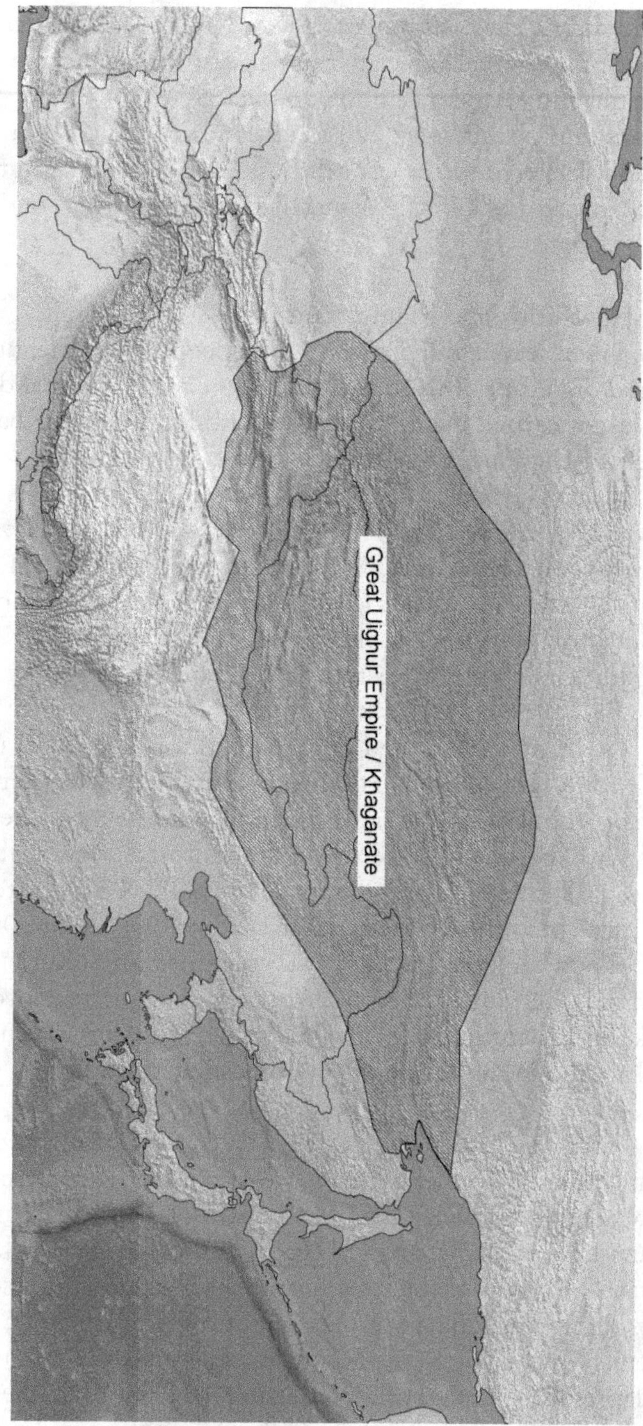

Figure 5: Map of the Great Uighur Empire / Khaganate

control of the Uighur Khaganate/Empire. The Uighur had essentially recreated the boundaries of the Xiongnu Empire. As with the Xiongnu and Gok-Turk, the Orkhon Valley of Mongolia became the Uighur center of power.

In 747 CE, the reins of power of the Uighur Khaganate passed to Bayanchur, the eldest son of Kutluk Bilge Khagan on the death of his father. Bayanchur Khan took the throne name of Khagan El Etimish Bilge (State settled, wise.) He astutely built trading posts with the Chinese and used the proceeds to build and fortify Ordu Baliq and expand the empire. His efforts brought many more peoples under the rule of the Uighur Empire.

With the An Lushan rebellion against the Tang beginning in 755, Emperor Xuanzong abdicated and fled to Sichuan. The army proclaimed Li Heng, his son, as Emperor Suzong (Su-tsung.) Tang Emperor Suzong (711 – 762 CE) called on the Uighur for military assistance in 756 and Bayanchur Khagan sent his eldest son at the head of a Uighur army to quell the insurrection. In return, he received the hand of a Chinese princess in marriage, Princess of Ning-kuo, daughter of the new Emperor. To cement their alliance, the Emperor took an Uighur princess as a wife. After the successful recapture of the capital of Loyang (757,) the Chinese showered the Uighur chiefs with many titles and gifts, including a promise of an annual shipment of 10,000 rolls of Chinese silks.

The fighting did not confine itself to the Central Kingdom as Bayanchur Khagan attacked the rival Yenisei Kyrgyz, another nomadic steppe tribe, to the north in 758. The Uighur destroyed several trading posts and the Kyrgyz responded by sending an army. The Kyrgyz khagan was among the casualties. The next year, 759 saw the death of Bayanchur and the rise of his second son, Yaghlagar Idigan as the new Uighur Khagan with the throne name of Tengri Khagan or Moyu Khagan.

The Chinese rebels once more captured Loyang and the Tang again called on the Uighur for assistance. Tengri Khagan initially started with his army to support the rebels and gain an easy victory over their southern neighbors. As fate would have it, a discussion with a Chinese diplomat changed his mind and instead he unseated the rebels in Loyang (762.) This decision would have a lasting effect on the Uighur Empire, for after his troops sacked the city, Tengri Khagan would remain in Loyang for a few months and encounter Manichaean missionaries. Four of the missionaries would return to Ordu Baliq with him early the next year and eventually convert him to the new religion. In 763 CE, the Khagan proclaimed for all his people to embrace the new religion.

Prior to Tengri Khagan's stay in Loyang, the Uighur worshipped Tengri, the Eternal Heavenly Father; but like the previous Gok-Turks, they tolerated other religious beliefs. Manicheanism was a Sogdian belief system, outlawed in Persia by the fire of a new religious fervor. Mani, the third century Persian prophet believed the teachings of the previous prophets, Buddha, Zoroaster, and Jesus did not encompass the complete understanding he had achieved in his revelations. He spoke of the struggle between good and evil, the world of spiritual light and the world of material darkness. Over the course of human history, the light would return from the material world, as humans sought and followed the spiritual path he laid out. On this course, the world would eventually transform into the spiritual light and eschew the material darkness. Historians also note he considered himself an apostle of Jesus. The Manichaean philosophy divided mankind into two broad categories; one of which was the clergy (called the elect,) lead by the supreme head with regional leaders similar to archbishops from the Church of Rome. The elects remained celibate, ate no meat and drank no fermented liquids. The other category was the auditors, the Manichaean laypeople. They had no dietary restrictions, but expected to be kind, generous in giving alms, and not overindulge in the consumption of food and beverage. Were they to fulfill their earthly duties, the auditors would reincarnate as an elect, leading mankind eventually to a world of light. Although a major religious influence from China to the Middle East, the Uighur Empire became the only state to proclaim Manicheanism a state religion.

The choice to follow the precepts of Mani's followers had a profound effect on the history and people of the Uighur Empire. Since the practice of Manicheanism, a 'western religion,' was almost just tolerated by the Chinese (who were Buddhists,) Tengri Khagan created a wedge to differentiate his people from the Chinese. To the Uighur Khagan, the rulers of the Central Kingdom were weak and feeble compared to his people. Tang dynasty China relied on the Uighur to overcome their internal political struggles, keep other barbarians at bay, and rewarded them handsomely. The tribute even continued despite an occasional raid on Chinese towns and villages. The Khagan realized if, as his Gok-Turk predecessors had done, his people aligned with the Chinese that they would ultimately lose their own identity. To maintain their independence from their southern neighbor, Tengri Khagan set his people on a path diametrically opposed to their philosophy and culture. Buddhism believes in cyclical existence and impermanence; there are no 'straight-line' beings existing from the beginning to the end of all creation. There is no eternal, omnipresent, omnipotent, omniscient being to answer prayers and intercede in human affairs. On the other hand, Tengri, the Heavenly Father, known to the nomads of the Orkhon Valley of Mongolia for centuries could be equated to the 'God' of Manichaeism. Additionally, the Mani Elect provided an organizational structure to turn his people towards a new, non-Chinese influenced society and impart lessons on living a new lifestyle.

Another factor in the selection of Sogdian allies was the financial acumen they brought to the table. The Sogdians had been trading goods along the Silk Road for centuries from Europe to China. The Uighur could now be privy to the secrets they held in the development of trade. When the Tang relied on the military assistance of the Uighur, the Uighur used their newfound knowledge to force an unfair trade with them. According to one Chinese historian, the Uighur provided tens of thousands of horses and the Chinese paid forty pieces of silk for each, even the useless ones. Some Uighur also moved to China, married and gained large amounts of land. They established their own money market and loaned money to be repaid with interest. These endeavors caused some angst, as this 'foreign' influence in finance and eventually in political circles supplanted Chinese control.

The inevitable outcome of the conversion to Manichaeism, whether planned or not, imposed changes on the nomadic Uighur lifestyle. Uighur nobles and others converting to the new faith eschewed the constant movement of yurts and herds to live in Ordu Baliq or Bai Baliq; planned, walled cities where yurts could be permanent and close to the Elect. Ordu Baliq and their cities were a departure from the traditional way of life. Rather than moving from place to place in search of fresh pastures and water, the Uighur 'progressed' to build a permanent capital, mimicking the sedentary lifestyle of their spiritual benefactors. Ordu Baliq had concentric walls and observation towers for security; fully fortified with troops to protect the people and goods contained therein. Storehouses within the walls contained all the goods a merchant might obtain, rather than just those a nomadic people might be able to store in an extra yurt and transport from pasture to pasture. The city was segregated; areas for handcrafts and trade were separated from the palace and temples.

Administration of the Empire required administrators and the creation of a permanent seat of government; the administrators needed to maintain awareness of the Khagan's location in case his counsel was required. These cities also served as centers of trade and commerce but signaled a decline in adherence to their nomadic tradition. Once the settled, the urban population became dependent on commodities produced elsewhere and was no longer required to perform extensive labor to produce their own food, they now had the opportunity to enrich their lives as never before. Agriculture expanded and literacy grew, albeit with Sogdian script. Artistic endeavors flourished as is seen by the images from the Bezeklik and Dunhuang caves discovered by Aurel Stein and others. These carefully crafted images of Uighur princes, nobles and the Manichean clergy in their fine silk clothing show they did not live the life of their nomadic ancestors. Of course, the changes brought about by urbanization were mostly felt closer to the cities and farther afield, the effects were less obvious.

The political influence of the Sogdian adherents of Mani injected itself into the decision-making process of the Uighur. In 779 CE, Tengri Khagan, as counseled by his Sogdian advisers, decided to take advantage of the enthronement of a new Tang emperor to invade the Central Kingdom. Perhaps Chinese intrigue caused his uncle, Tun Bagha, to take decisive action and assassinate his nephew before the plot unfolded. Tun Bagha became the fourth Khagan of the Uighur and took the throne name Alp Qutlugh Bilge (Victorious, Glorious, Wise.) Along with the former Khagan, Tun Bagha's rise to power also included the murder of many of Tengri Khagan's Sogdian allies and a marked shift away from the influence of the Manichaeism clergy. The new Emperor Dezong (Te-tsung) (742 – 805 CE) rewarded the new Khagan with a real Chinese princess, his daughter; Princess of Hsien-an. Tun Bagha changed the rules back and again brought the Yenesei Kyrgyz under the control of the Khaganate. His ten-year reign ended at his death and his eldest son, throne name Ai Tengride Bulmish Kulug Bilge ascended the throne only to be killed a year later by his younger brother. The rebellion that followed was quick and seated the former Khagan's son, almost still a child, on the throne instead of the attempted usurper. His throne name was Qutlugh Bilge and his time on the throne was marked by decline. His armies were unable to prevent the Tibetans and Karluks from seizing Uighur territory and he could no longer maintain a grip on his empire. He only reigned for five years, ending the Yaghlakar dynasty in 795 CE.

After the death of Tun Bagha, Sogdian influence began to be felt again, culminating in 807 CE with the first Uighur embassy to include Manichaeans to visit the Tang capital, Chang'An (Xian.) The new Khagan, first ruler of the Ediz dynasty, assumed the throne in 795 CE (throne name Ai Tengride Ulug Bulmish Alp Qutlugh Ulugh Bilge,) and rolled back the constraints on the religion of Mani, turning away again from Chinese influences. The new Khagan, a former general, used the reins of power to reconsolidate the empire and start the new dynasty. Known as one of the greatest monarchs of the Uighur, he brought about a great restoration of the empire and some of his accomplishments outlasted his reign ending in 808 CE. His successor, the eighth Uighur Khagan, took the same throne name as his predecessor and ruled until 820 CE. During his reign, he commissioned the Karabalghasun inscription in Old Turkic, Sogdian and Chinese scripts to record the history of the Uighur. Unfortunately, the Uighur Empire had seen its better days.

One explanation for the weakening of the empire could point to the civilizing effect of the conversion to Manicheanism. The newly urbanized sector of the population no longer related to their former lifestyle and the prosecution of war became distasteful. The social and political separation between the urban peoples and those outside their direct influence is another factor enhancing instability. Local officials could decide to ignore the

Khagan's orders and set their own agendas; this division proved an overwhelming obstacle to the continuation of the empire.

The decline continued for the last twenty years (820 – 840 CE) of the Uighur Empire. The Yenisei Kyrgyz to the north restarted hostilities in 820 and continued intermittently for the next twenty years. The Kyrgyz used the disunity among Uighurs to their advantage, even inviting Uighur generals to defect to their side. The silk/horse trade with the Chinese appears to have ceased after 829 leading to a further weakening of the empire. Chinese records relate in 839 that massive famine and pestilence struck the Uighur and heavy snowfalls further complicated the situation. In 840, the Kyrgyz accepted the invitation of a rebel Uighur chief to march against the Khagan and arrived in strength. After capturing Ordu Baliq and killing the Khagan, the Uighur were forced to disperse. The Great Uighur Empire was finished.

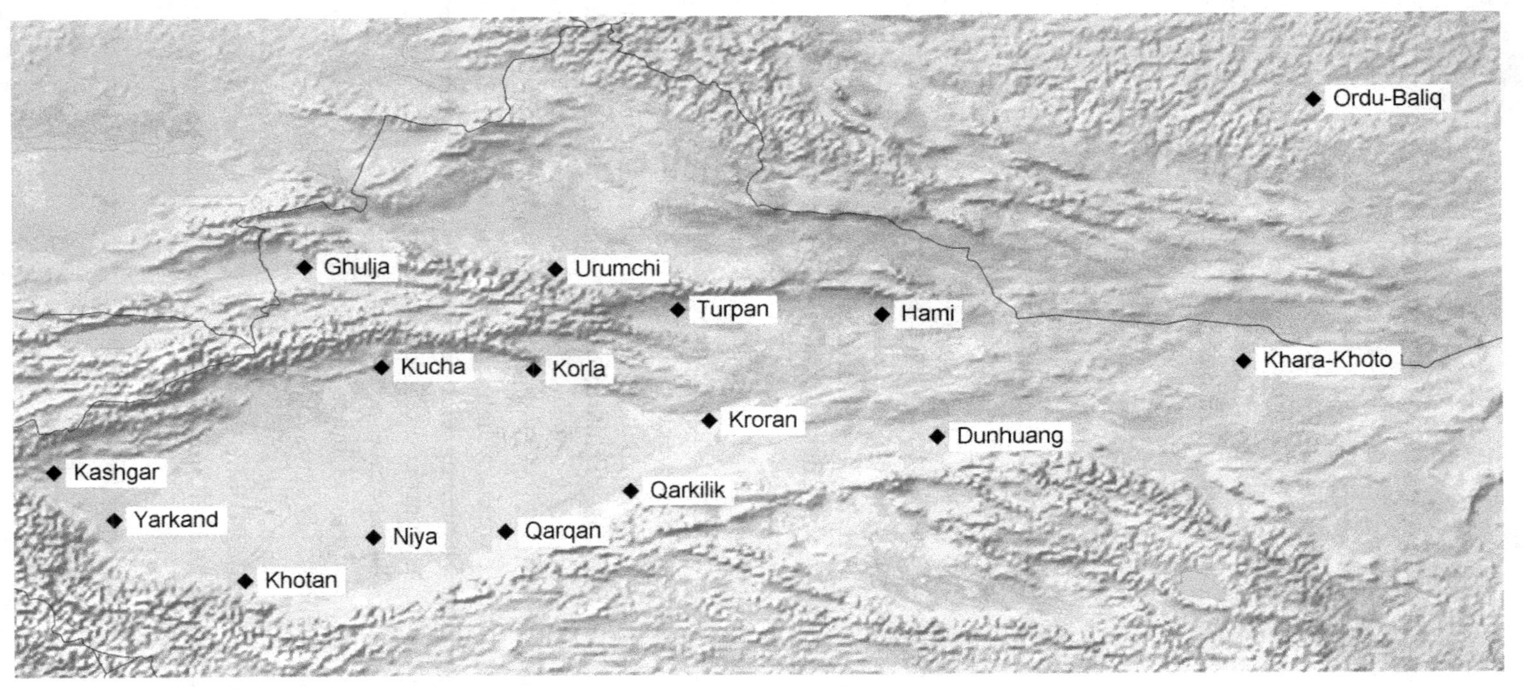
Ordu-Baliq
Ghulja
Urumchi
Turpan
Hami
Kucha
Korla
Khara-Khoto
Kroran
Dunhuang
Kashgar
Qarkilik
Yarkand
Niya
Qarqan
Khotan

Figure 6: Cites of the Tarim Basin

Chapter 3: Legacy of the Great Uighur Empire

Subsequent to the collapse of the Great Uighur Empire/Khaganate, the Uyghur migrated primarily into Tang China around Shanshi province with lesser numbers migrating westward to either the Tarim Basin or to what is now known as Gansu in China.

Gansu Uighur Kingdom

The 'Yughurs' as their descendants are sometimes known, formed the Gansu Uighur Kingdom in the Hexi Corridor lasting from 894 – 1036 CE. A community of the Uighur had settled in the area before the collapse of their Khaganate and descendants of the Yaghlakar clan once again claimed the leadership over the new kingdom. While most of the borders of the Tarim Basin surrounding the Taklamakan desert are mountainous, on the eastern end is the Hexi Corridor, allowing unfettered access to China. Perched on one end of the Silk Road, the Uighur built a new kingdom with their new neighbors. As many became Buddhist, much effort went into the development of religious infrastructure where the faithful could meditate and increase their knowledge. The images painted on the walls of the 492 temples carved into the caves known as the Thousand Buddha Grottoes or the Mogao Grottoes depict pantheons of Buddhist deities as well as images of the wealthy Uighur patrons financing the elaborate displays. Near Dunhuang, Gansu, there are at least five of these great collections of art and religion stretching back to 366 CE. The discovery of a 'library cave' provided the world with thousands of manuscripts written in Chinese, Sanskrit, Sogdian, Old Uyghur, Hebrew, Tibetan, Tangut, and Old Turkic. These ancient documents, collectively known as the Dunhuang Manuscripts are an invaluable source for researchers of Central Asian history, art and religion. The range of languages contained in the documents indicates cross-cultural ties with other civilizations thousands of miles away.

Eventually, the Tangut Western Xia (Hsia) Dynasty absorbed the Gansu Uighur kingdom in 1036.

The Tangut (also known as Qiang) people, originally from what is known as Qinghai and Sichuan (northeastern Tibet) migrated northward before the 10th century into northwestern China. Originally, their capital was Yinchuan and located in the Ningxia Autonomous Region of the Peoples Republic of China. Another of their cities, Khara-Khoto, was a center of trade in the 11th century and has been the subject of many wondrous tales.

In 1210, the Tangut Ruler submitted to the Great Khan (Chinggis Khan) (1162-1227 CE) as a vassal state with the understanding he would send troops to aid in future military campaigns when asked. After the Shah of Khwarazmia rebuffed a peaceful mission from the "Ruler of All in Felt Tents" and a subsequent Mongol emissary lost his head, Chinggis Khan asked for assistance from the Tangut to field his army of retribution for the major insult. Their refusal was noted and after a two-year campaign (1219-1221 CE,) where estimates place over 25% of the population (or 1.25 million) of Khwarazmia were killed, attention was turned to the Western Xia. The death of the Khan during the attack on Yinchuan exacerbated the brutality of the Mongol conquest that extinguished most of the Western Xia. Although a major city in the Western Xia kingdom, Khara-khoto did not suffer the destruction unleashed upon the other Tangut cities, towns and villages by Chinggis Khan's armies. Marco Polo, a later visitor to Kublai Khan in the 13th century, wrote in *The Travels of Marco Polo* about the city of Edzina or Etzina, identified as Khara-khoto:

> When you leave the city of Campichu you ride for twelve days, and then reach a city called Etzina, which is towards the north on the verge of the Sandy Desert; it belongs to the Province of Tangut. The people are Idolaters, and possess plenty of camels and cattle, and the country produces a number of good falcons, both Sakers and Lanners. The inhabitants live by their cultivation and their cattle, for they have no trade. At this city you must needs lay in victuals for forty days, because when you quit Etzina, you enter on a desert which extends forty days'

journey to the north, and on which you meet with no habitation nor baiting-place.
The Travels of Marco Polo

In 1372, a Northern Yuan general, his troops and a caravan of treasure sought refuge in the city from the soldiers of the Chinese Ming dynasty. Four years earlier, the Chinese revolted and retook their country from the Mongols. They formed the Ming Dynasty and drove the previous Yuan dynasty back to Mongolia. The siege on Khara-khoto brought defeat for those in the city, but differing accounts relate differing outcomes. In one retelling, Ming troops diverted the flow of the Ejin River to deprive the city of water and eventual capitulation when the Mongol leader, Buyan Temurn eventually surrendered. Another story tells of the vast amount of wealth buried somewhere inside the city and how the leader murdered his family and committed suicide while his troops faced the final onslaught of the Chinese. The only version with a happy conclusion to the story relates the Mongols broke through the twelve-foot walls and escaped through the desert to safety. This ending has some evidence for its veracity, as a breach in the wall still exists where riders can pass. The legends relate the abandonment of the city thereafter and the entire region came under Chinese control.

Kingdom of Qocho (Idiqut State, Uighuristan)

The other major portion of the westward migration of the remnants of the Great Uighur Empire saw them continue into the Tarim Basin. Following a descendant of the Ediz clan, they formed the Kingdom of Qocho (Kocho,) also known as the Idiqut State or Uighuristan, lasting from 843 to the mid-thirteenth century. The kingdom had Kara-Khoja as its winter capital near present-day Turpan and they summered north of the Tian Shan Mountains at Beshbalik, known to the Chinese as Beiting (Peiting.) They knew the people they encountered in their new lands, as the Uighur had maintained control prior to the collapse of their previous empire. Their new neighbors were a sedentary Indo-European people professing devotion to Mahayana Buddhism and speaking a tongue known as Tocharian. In the next centuries, the Turkic Uighur language overcame the Indo-European Tocharian as the common tongue, but on the other hand, the once stalwart Manichaeans gradually gave into the allure of Buddhism. Additionally, the kingdom adopted the Sogdian script and created their own alphabet, known as Old Uighur.

The Bezeklik 'Thousand Buddha' grottoes, started in the fifth century by the Tocharians, eventually expanded into seventy-seven caverns carved into solid rock. Adorned by images of the Buddhas, Bodhisattvas, and patrons of the gifted artists, the artwork provides a clear picture of the assimilation of the two peoples into a unified sedentary Turkic culture.

Islam spread to their western neighbors, the Qarakanid (Kara-Khanid) Khanate, after the conversion of Satuq Bughra Khan in 934. Speaking of the Idiqut State, Uyghur scholar Mahmud Kashgari (1005-1102 CE) wrote:

> The State of Uyghur has five cities. Their people are the most ferocious infidels and the most skillful shooters. Those cities are Solmi, which Zulqarnäyin let them build, Qochu, Jan Baliq, Bäsh Baliq, and Yengi Baliq

In 1130 CE, the Kingdom of Qocho became a vassal state under the Qara Khitai and less than 100 years later (1209 CE), their ruler, Baurchuk Art Tekin, declared his allegiance to Chinggis Khan and became vassals of the Mongol Empire. The sedentary, urbanized Uighur assumed the role of administrators in service to the empire of the Great Khan, as the Mongols still maintained a nomadic lifestyle. A little more than 160 years later (1370 CE,) the Qocho Kingdom disintegrated into the Chagatai Khanate, one successor to the Great Mongol Empire, originally led by the second son of Chinggis Khan, Chagatai (1183 – 1242 CE.)

The conversion of the Buddhist cities of the Tarim Basin to Islam started in the 10th century after the conversion of Sultan Satug Bughra Khan. According to Peter Golden, author of the chapter entitled Karakhanids and Early Islam in the *Cambridge History of Early Inner Asia* (edited by Denis Sinor,) the major impetus for the conversion to Islam was not jihad or use of military force to convert the Inner Asian steppe peoples. Muslim merchant caravans and settlers seeking new markets brought Islam along with them and provided new goods and services. To embrace all the benefits offered by the newcomers, there were economic and societal pressures to convert, rather than a forced conversion. Another factor was the mystic Sufis who preached and propagated the new faith from village to village. Their description as dynamic and charismatic, resembling the Turkic shamans, won many converts with their fiery rhetoric. Islamization was complete in the fifteenth century.

The descendants of the Great Uighur Empire and the states formed by their people maintained the role as an enlightening influence in Inner Asia. As evidenced by the tens of thousands of documents known as the Dunhuang manuscripts, we know the Uighur were gifted artists and musicians, religious and secular scholars. They communicated with countries far and wide and learned how to make the desert bloom and feed their populations. As a tolerant society, they accepted people of all faiths and creeds (with a few exceptions.) The Uighur are a shining example of the positive transformation of a people from a pastoral lifestyle to urban city dwellers with a high standard of living. This is one legacy of the Great Uighur Empire.

Chapter 4: The Uyghur

According to some scholars, there is no connection between the people of the Great Uighur Khaganate / Empire and the people living around the Tarim Basin today. They insist the Uighur people disappeared after the collapse of their empire; losing their cultural identity amid all the other peoples of Central Asia. Other scholars point to the continuous occupation of the descendants of the Great Uighur Empire around the Tarim Basin. They point out how the people adapted and developed their cultural identity over the centuries along the north and south legs of the Silk Road. Using the later definition, the Taklamakanians, or the Turkic inhabitants of the Tarim Basin and surrounding areas are part of a continuously developing culture stretching back to the second millennium BCE. The desiccated corpses of the Caucasian Tocharians released from beneath the deserts sands of the Taklamakan are carbon-dated from 2000 BCE to 600 CE. These people joined with refugees from the Uighur Khaganate to create the Idiqut State and the Gansu Uighur Kingdom. As mentioned previously, the fusion of their cultures produced a new Turkic identity and their descendants still live there today.

In excavations of the ancient kingdom of Kroran (Loulan,) artifacts dating from the Bronze Age (3300 – 1200 BCE) through the Iron Age (1500 – 200 BCE) have revealed priceless evidence of their early way of life. Located on the eastern edge of the Taklamakan between Dunhuang and Korla, Kroran was a way station on the northern branch of the Silk Road. The city was inhabited beginning in the second century BCE and lasted until the sixth century CE when the remaining inhabitants immigrated northeast to Hami. DNA studies of the earliest inhabitants indicate a link with the Eastern Mediterranean and the Afanasevo culture discussed earlier. The dry sands of the Taklamakan have preserved many of the items that in other climates would have disintegrated over the centuries. From some of the tombs already excavated, archaeologists have unearthed woolen textiles, multi-colored robes, trousers, boots, stockings, coats, felt hats, golden ornaments, and implements of wood, bone and horn. Along with stone arrowheads and bronze and iron knives, examples of their pottery vessels such as serving containers, cooking ware, bowls, and drinking receptacles have shown them to be a sedentary people, relying on agriculture and animal husbandry.

North of Kroran, was the kingdom of Turpan, also inhabited by peoples speaking Indo-European languages and related to the same peoples as lived in Kroran. They were also a way station on the northern Silk Road. Their capital city, Yarghul (Chinese: Jiaohe) dates from the third century BCE and is located six miles west of present-day Turpan. In the fifth century CE, the capital moved to nearby Idiqut, eventually becoming a walled city with a circumference of 3 miles. The city became the capital of the Idiqut state as previously discussed after the influx of the Uighur people in the ninth century CE. The excavations at Yarghul yielded precious artifacts such as paper documents, wooden figurines, silk paintings, Roman and Persian coins and just like Kroran, the remains of ancient foods still prepared in the same manner today by the Taklamakanians. Evidence of the preparation of Nan (bread,) dumplings, and kawaps (Kebabs) indicate these foods have a long and storied history among the inhabitants of the Tarim Basin.

An ancient city along the southwestern portion of the Tarim Basin is Khotan. Located along the older, southern route of the Silk Road, Khotan was established in the third century BCE. From Khotan, merchants could travel further west to China or southerly to India and Tibet, a crossroads where the exchange of goods, philosophies, technologies and religions carried on for millennia. DNA analysis of the mummies unearthed from near Khotan indicates the same Indo-European people settled here and maintained a sedentary lifestyle. Khotan is renowned for the quality of jade discovered nearby and Chinese records identify Khotan as the source of jade in ancient China.

At the westernmost end of the Tarim Basin lies the ancient city of Kashgar. At the crossroad for the north and south routes of the Silk Road, Kashgar was an important trading center. Twenty miles northeast of Kashgar is another ancient walled city buried beneath the sand, believed started in the third century BCE and lasting until the thirteenth century. The remains of the houses sheltering the faithful, Buddhist temples and pagodas, and some city walls still poke from the desert; the location even boasts an underground water system like the one still used in Turpan. Mahmud Kashgari, author of the *Compendium of the Languages of the Turks*, hailed from Kashgar and his work continues to enhance the study of history of the Turkic people. As the other ancient cities previously mentioned, the early inhabitants were Indo-Europeans, eventually becoming 'Turkicised' by the Uighur and other Turkic peoples.

With just a small portion of the ruins so far uncovered, further great discoveries are on the horizon to enhance our knowledge and understanding of the history of the people and the lives they lead around one of the most hostile environments on earth. Already the glimpse provided by archaeological discovery indicates the inhabitants of the Tarim Basin, the Taklamakanians, inherit a rich, vibrant culture built on over thousands of years of history.

The Taklamakanians are the Uyghur, with a rich history including their past as members of the Great Uighur Empire. It is unique among the myriad of cultures and peoples populating our planet. The Uyghur made a desert fertile and built a civilization comparable to any other on Earth, yet, as a 'Chinese minority,' today they face an uncertain future.

The Chinese Communist Party ruled People's Republic of China attempts to assert a claim on the historic land of the Taklamakanians based on their presence in the region during the Han Dynasty (206 BCE – 220 CE.) Their claim falls flat when we examine the subsequent history of the region. After the Tang Dynasty retreated from the region in the eighth century CE, Central Asia was no longer under the control of a Chinese state, if you consider the Mongols (Yuan dynasty) and the Manchurians (Qing dynasty) were foreign (non-Chinese) conquerors. The master of the Tarim Basin between 1865 and 1877 was Tajik adventurer Yakub Beg, the Amir of Kashgar. It was not until 1876 that the Qing sent an army lead by a Chinese general to conquer the region. The name 'Xinjiang' or "New Dominion" replaced the previous East or Chinese Turkestan after General Zhou succeeded in his conquest.

After the collapse of the Qing in 1912, the newly created Republic of China maintained a tenuous hold on the region. The first Republic of East Turkestan formed in 1933 and lasted a year until Hui warlords aligned with the Republic of China sacked their capital of Kashgar. The Second Republic of East Turkestan (1944-1949) ended soon after the plane carrying the leaders of the Republic crashed on the way to Beijing for negotiations with the new People's Republic of China. Subsequently, forces of the Peoples Liberation Army subjugated the land and its people.

Although promised autonomy and guaranteed specific rights under the constitution of the People's Republic of China, laws and regulations prohibit teaching in the Uyghur language in schools. Prohibitions exist on Muslim men wearing beards or women wearing the hijab in public; regulations force Uyghur restaurants to remain open and lunch is mandatory for office workers during the Ramadan daylight fast. The Uyghur people are singled out for the confiscation of their passports. Families with overseas relatives are persecuted to coerce their return or silence their criticism of the situation in their homeland. News accounts of the continuing clampdown on the Uyghur people regularly appear and recently tell of the confinement of hundreds of thousands of Uyghur and other Turkic peoples in re-education camps. Having a relative express a desire to travel abroad is one of the reasons for re-education and long-term confinement.

The process of cultural assimilation (and the extinction of Uyghur culture and language except in old books and videos,) underlies the policies of the Chinese communists in the Peoples Republic of China. The same is being foisted on the Mongols and Tibetans in order to maintain the primacy of the dictatorship of the people, the Chinese Communist Party.

In 1949, after the Chinese communist takeover, the population in East Turkestan/Xinjiang was 76% Uyghur. After decades of population transfers, they have become a minority in their own land. According to the official 2015 Chinese government population statistics, the Uyghur made up 45.84% of the total population of Xinjiang at 23.6 million. This official figure turns out to be 10.82 million people, but others place the count higher. That is more than any country in Central America except for Mexico and Guatemala; more than any country in Northern Europe other than the United Kingdom. There are more Uyghur in the People's Republic of China than Austrians, Danes, or the Swiss; and yet as a 'minority,' they are facing the extinction of their culture, language, and lifestyle. If we, as citizens of Earth, have learned anything over the past four-hundred years, certainly the obliteration of indigent peoples, cultures, and languages to impose a foreign sense of modernity is a crime against humanity.

Is Eastern Turkestan a Chinese Territory?

From: Common Voice, the publication of The Allied Committee of the Peoples of Eastern Turkestan, Inner Mongolia, and Tibet Volume 1 1988

By Erkin Alptekin

During an interview with the correspondent of the Beijing Review, Wang Enmao, first secretary of Eastern Turkestan Party Committee, claims that:

> "In the early days of liberation, some people suggested we copy the Soviet method of establishing a union of republics in China. But our circumstances are different from those of the Soviet Union, which became a union of republics only after the October Revolution with the gradual merging of 14 republics with Russia. China has been a united state since ancient times. How could it go backwards to a federal system to establish a union of republics?"(1)

It is true that in the early days of the so-called liberation, the people of Eastern Turkestan pleaded that they might be permitted at least to form a federated republic in China. While doing this, they were relying on the promises of the Chinese Communists made before seizing power in China. The Provisional Constitution of the Chinese Worker-Peasant Democratic Republic, approved by the First All-China Congress of Workers and Peasants Deputies in 1931, proclaimed:

> "In such regions as Mongolia, Tibet, Sinkiang... the nationalities have the right to determine by themselves whether they want to secede from the Chinese Soviet Republic and form their independent states, or to join the Union..., or to form autonomous regions within the Chinese Soviet Republic."(2)

At the Seventh Congress in 1945, Mao Tsetung, in his report on coalition government, having denounced the Kuomintang's oppressive policies as those of great chauvinism, said that the Communists fully endorse the nationality problem, which was to grant them "self-determination" after the Communist takeover in China.(3)

But after he seized power in China, Mao completely denied his "self-determination" promises.
Faced with this situation, the people of Eastern Turkestan pleaded that they might be permitted at least to form a federated republic. But Mao rejected this request on the following grounds:

> "For two thousand years Sinkiang has been an inalienable part of an indivisible China; therefore, there would be no sense in dividing China into federated republics; this is a demand hostile to history and to socialism."(4)

Wang Enmao, the first secretary of Eastern Turkestan Party Committee, is now repeating the same argument. This is not something new. In order to justify their domination of Eastern Turkestan, the Chinese have always claimed that this country was annexed to China two thousand years ago, that the Chinese dwelled in this territory and therefore, Eastern Turkestan is an indivisible part of China.

This distorts the historical facts. If we examine neutral historical sources we come to a completely different conclusion than that given by Chinese sources which are mostly written from a Chinese point of view to protect Chinese interests.

The well-known western scholar and sinologist Prof. Wolfram Eberhard claims that the Chinese sources give one-sided information, so it is necessary to check other sources before coming to a final conclusion concerning the history of China's neighbouring peoples in ancient times.(5)

It is true that in order to control the Silk Road, China staged invasions of Eastern Turkestan in 104 B.C., 59 B.C., 73 A.D., 448 A.D., 657 A.D., and 744 A.D.(6) But the first invasion was thwarted by the peoples of Eastern Turkestan in 86 B.C., the second in 10 B.C., the third in 102 A.D., the fourth in 460 A.D., the fifth in 699 A.D. and the last one in 751 A.D.(7) Thus, over a period of 855 years Eastern Turkestan was invaded six times by the Chinese, and if we add up these six invasions, the total period of Chinese occupation of Eastern Turkestan was only 157 years. It must also be said that during these 157 years China could not establish a complete control over Eastern Turkestan because of continued resistance.(8) Outside of these 157 years of Chinese occupation, Eastern Turkestan remained a free and independent country for 698 years.(9)

After the last defeat of the Chinese by the combined forces of Arabs, Turkic peoples and the Tibetans in 751 A.D., a period of 1,000 years passed until the conquest of Eastern Turkestan by the Manchus, if we discount Mongol rule in Eastern Turkestan(10) Mongol rule cannot be accepted as a Chinese domination of Eastern Turkestan, because the Uighurs, a Turkic people, voluntarily joined the Mongol Empire, maintained their sovereignty, and played an important role throughout the empire's history.(11) On the other hand, during Mongol rule a racial law was adopted, according to which the Chinese were treated as the lowest caste in the empire with no rights whatsoever.(12)

The Manchus, who set up a huge empire in China, invaded Eastern Turkestan in 1759, and dominated it until 1862. During this period the people of Eastern Turkestan revolted 42 times against the Manchu rule with the purpose of regaining their independence.(13) In the last revolt of 1863, the people of Eastern Turkestan were successful in expelling the Manchus from their motherland, and founded an independent state under the leadership of Yakub Beg Badavlat. This state was recognised by the Ottoman Empire, Tsarist Russia and Great Britain.(14)

In the fear of a Tsarist Russian expansion into Eastern Turkestan, large forces under the overall command of General Zho Zhung Tang attacked Eastern Turkestan in 1876. After this invasion, Eastern Turkestan was given the name Sinkiang, and it was annexed into the Manchu Empire on 18 November 1884.(15) This means, Eastern Turkestan was conquered during the rule of the Manchus. But before conquering Eastern Turkestan they conquered China. The Manchus were foreigners not only to the Eastern Turkestanis but also to the Chinese. When the Manchu rule in China was overthrown, Eastern Turkestan should have become free also. But the Chinese raised claims on Eastern Turkestan, though it had been conquered by their own conquerors.

It must also be said that long before the Chinese invasion took place, in 539 B.C., Eastern Turkestan was invaded by the Iranic peoples; in 330 B.C. by Alexander the Great; and twice in 670 A.D.

and 789 A.D. by the Tibetans.(16) Obviously, this means that none of the historic and forgotten invasions constitute a base for territorial claims today. Otherwise, the, Turkic peoples, Tibetans and the Mongols could raise territorial claims on parts of China as well.

It is a historical fact that pre-historic dynasties like the Shang (1450-1050 B.C.) Chou (1050-247 B.C.) and Chin (247-206 B.C.) were founded by non-Chinese peoples such as proto-Turk, proto-Tibetan and proto-Mongol peoples.(17) This means that in ancient times, China was ruled by non-Chinese peoples for 1203 years.

In the Middle Ages, that is between 220 A.D. and 1280 a total of 1060 years China was ruled for 740 years by Turkic, Mongol and Tungusic, peoples.(18) During this period the Chinese were able to rule their own country for 540 years, but were unable to control the whole of the Chinese territory because of wars with non-Chinese peoples, as well as interior rebellions and court intrigues.(19)

In more recent times, that is between 1280 and 1911--which is a total of 631 years--the Chinese were able to rule their own country for only 276 years.(20) In this period, the non-Chinese peoples ruled China for 355 years.(21)

Only during the reign of the Han dynasty(206 B.C.--220 A.D.) were the Chinese able to rule themselves; but they were constantly threatened by the Hsing-nu or the Hun, against whom the Chinese erected the Great Wall. With this Great Wall, for the first time in history the boundaries were marked between the Chinese--the settled people--and the non-Chinese--the nomadic people.(22) The Great Wall is the best proof that Eastern Turkestan was always outside Chinese territory. One of the western gates of the Great Wall is named Yu Min Guang. This gate faces Eastern Turkestan. Eastern Turkestan is famous for its precious stone, Jade. In the New China Atlas, which was published in 1939 in Shanghai, it is clearly indicated that during the Ch'in Dynasty (256 B.C.--206 B.C.), during the Han Dynasty (206 B.C.--220 A.D.) and during the Tang Dynasty (618 A.D.--907 A.D.) the Jade gate was accepted by the Chinese as their westernmost border.(23)

Thus over a period of 3361 year of Chinese history, the Chinese ruled their own country for only 1242, and for the remaining period of 2119 years China was ruled by non-Chinese peoples such as the Turkics, Tibetans, Mongols and the Manchus.

The ancient Chinese emperors regarded themselves as the "sons of heaven." Thus, all countries in the world were Chinese "sovereignties". Under these circumstances, no "boundaries existed" for the Chinese.(24) The later Chinese rulers could not disengage themselves from this view.

One of the first Chinese traveler, Fa Hsien, who visited the cities of Turfan, Karashehir, Kucha, Hoten and Charkalik in 399 A.D., writes in his memoirs that during his trip to Eastern Turkestan he met no Chinese.(25) Another traveler, Hsuan Chang, who followed the same route in 629 A.D. confirms Fa Hsein's words, and writes in his memoirs that during his trip to Eastern Turkestan he met only three Chinese monks.(26) This suggests that until the conquest of Eastern Turkestan by the Manchu rulers of China in 1759, there were no Chinese settlement in the country. Even if there had been Chinese settlements, this should not have justified territorial claims on Eastern Turkestan. Today there are millions of Chinese living in the United States, Europe and South East Asian countries. Does that mean that these countries belong to China?

Pan Ku, the great historian of the Han Dynasty (206 B.C.--220 A.D.) writes the following:

"As for clothing, costume, food and language, the barbarians are entirely different from the Middle Kingdom... Mountains, valleys and the great desert separate them from us, This barrier which lies between the interior and the alien was made by heaven and earth. Therefore, the sage rulers considered them as beasts and neither established contact with them nor subjugated them... the land is impossible to cultivate and the people are impossible to rule as subjects. Therefore, they are always to be considered as outsiders and never as citizens... Our administration and teaching have never reached their people..."(27)

Not only do these words prove that during the Han Dynasty, Eastern Turkestan was not under Chinese "administration", but the people of Eastern Turkestan was always regarded as "outsiders", not as "citizens" and the Chinese "teaching" never reached them.

China should not justify their possession of this land by distorting historical fact.

NOTES

1. Beijing Review, December 17, 1984.
2. East Turkic Review, No 4, Munich 1960, p. 94.
3. Mao Zedong, Selected Works, Moscow 1953, p. 549-555.
4. Narinbayev, Kommunizm Tugi, August 1, 1974,
5. Wofram Eberhard, Cinin Simali Komsulari, Ankara 1942, p. 2.
6. Ibid, History of China, Ankara 1947, p. 93-109; 0wen Lattimore, Pivor of Asia, Boston 1950, p. 45-46; Jack Chen, The Sinkiang Story, London 1977, p. 21, 23; M.E. Bugra, Dogu Turkistan Hurriyet Davasi ve Cin Siyaseti, Istanbul 1955, p. 24.
7. Ibid.
8. Ibid.
9. Ibid,
10. Ibid.
11. von Gabain, Das Leben im Uighurischen Konigreich von Qoco, Wiesbaden 1973, p. 19.
12. Wolfram Eberhard, Ibid. p. 259-270; Henry Schwarz, Chinas Development Experience. New York 1916 p. 196.
13. M.E. Bupra, Ibid.
14. IY, Alptekin, Dogu Turkistan Davasi, Istanbul 1973, p. 126-128.
15. Owen Lattimore, Ibid, p. 50.
16. von Gabain, Ibid, p. 20.
17. Wolfram Eberhard, Ibid,ip. 31, 33, 78.
18. Ibid.
19. Ibid.
20. Ibid, p. 257-258.
21. Ibid,i
22. Owen Lattimore, Studies in Frontier History, London 1962, p. 59.
23. Chinas New Atlas, Shanghai 1939 p. 51; also see Herman Albert Historical and Commercial AtIas of China, Harvard University Press, 1935.
24. Wolfram Eberhard, Ibid, p. 41.
25. von Gabain, Ibid, p. 20; I. Musabay-P. Turfani, Turk Dunyasi EI Kitabi, Istanbul 1976, p. 1226; Herman Albert, Ibid.
26. Ibid.

27. Pan Ku, "The Account of Hsing-nu," Han-shu, 91, sect. 2 p. 32 a-b.

Part 2: Other Depictions of the Great Uighur Empire

Chapter 1: Tales, Legends and Mysteries of Long-Forgotten Places

When I saw the Uyghur language copy of the Lost Continent of Mu arrive in my mailbox, my interest in researching my great-grandfather's theories was again piqued. This was another side to my Uyghur friends I had not yet seen. I had done quite a bit of reading Central Asian history and did not understand how my great-grandfather's theories could be of interest. Of course, I was unable to read the Uyghur language version. Thankfully, English language versions were available in paperback book sales outlets and all over the internet to enable me to explore my newfound interest.

Some Uyghur friends explained the interest in James Churchward's theories as a modern-day mythology for the Uyghur people. In the ninety years since his first book went into circulation, other peoples had incorporated James' story of the Great Uighur Empire into their nationalist mythos. Some Hungarian authors declare their connection as descendants from the culturally advanced ancient Uighur. Turkish authors proclaim the 'Turkishness' of the Uighur and claim them as their ancestors. Some New Agers also include the Uighur as the civilizing force over all the 'lesser' peoples of our planet, some hinting this history also sets them above everyone else. Eventually, the people named in James' fantastic accounts of Uighur pseudo-history became aware of these new versions of history. The story line provided hope for a different future from the day-to-day realities of life under the 'dictatorship of the people,' the Chinese Communist Party. After decades of propaganda and prosecution for their unique heritage, the new mythos provided a sense of optimism and confidence in their identity.

The Uyghur language version is not the only translated version of the Lost Continent of Mu; versions exist in French, Russian and probably a few more I have not seen. It would be foolish to believe a completely faithful translation in any other language exists. In some cases, an inadvertent word choice slightly modifies the text to convey a different meaning; in other cases, such as the Russian, the released version mimics the original in tone and style while modifying the contents to match propaganda goals and/or the politics of the translator. One change in the Russian language edition was brought to my attention when visiting with an Uyghur member of Elle Ayat from Kazakhstan. Some of his first questions posed were about what James wrote about the Uighur Empire and some of the basic information was different from that contained in his books. In whatever manner people change James' original writings, each version needs scrutiny to uncover James' true meaning and intent.

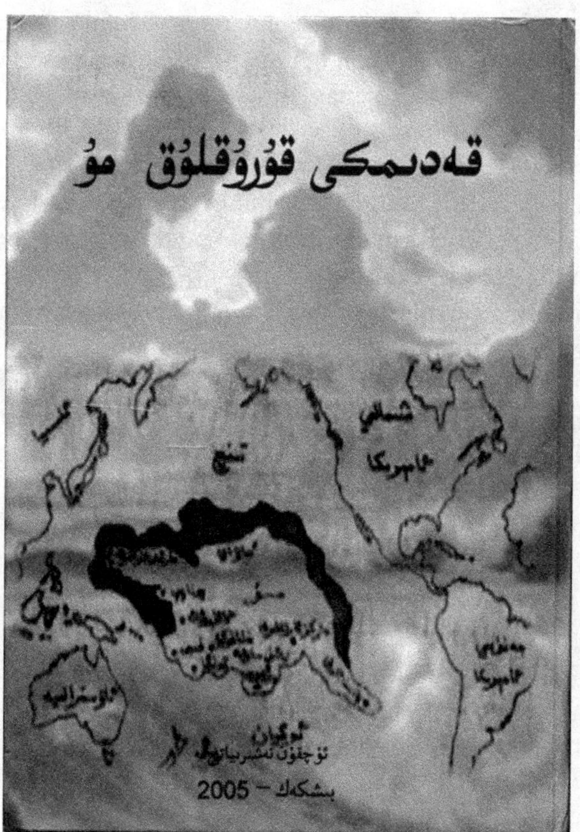

Figure 7: Cover of Uyghur language *Lost Continent of Mu*

The steppes of Inner Asia, as with other remote places, provide the backdrop for fanciful tales and some unique interpretations of history. Legends such as the cache of Mongol riches buried in the ruins of isolated Khara-khoto, or the community of enlightened masters living in the hidden valley of Shambala in Tibet excites the imagination and inspires the soul. Apart from the curriculum taught in school or Sunday school, these tales weave a new complexity into our reality and creates a new sense of possibilities for our future. Perhaps the lost riches of Khara-khoto contain some clue to another overlooked great treasure or documents providing valuable insight to a treatment for an unsolvable medical affliction. Or maybe the enlightened Masters of Shambala would pass along some great wisdom to bring our world into harmony, or whisper to us the secret of a long, healthy life. These new possibilities become the inspiration for a hopeful future and satisfy our hunger to create a better understanding about our own human journey.

However, the evaluation of the veracity of these tales, fables or myths is necessary to gain the proper understanding and/or to set the appropriate goals. Otherwise, it may set one on a fool's errand. Sometimes an author picks up a dubious news item and constructs some new tale; these, most assuredly, should be regarded as fiction. One case in point is James' tale of the Great Uighur Empire, discussed in subsequent paragraphs.

Other legends are the product of many retellings. On one hand, these stories perhaps contain at their core at least some fact or legend; expanded, expounded upon, and reiterated around a thousand campfires for centuries. The legend always grows at each retelling and it is up to the listener to discern between fact and fantasy. On the other hand, the fable may be fiction from the start. A lack of historical knowledge sometimes leads to confusion concerning where to draw the line between fact and fantasy. In some instances, there is no effort to filter the real from the fantastic or the account purposely maintains focus on the untenable to support the author's agenda. Unfortunately, the truth escapes these presentations; denying the reader an opportunity to make a fair judgement.

The critical examination of these tales requires a general historical understanding and extraordinary proofs for extraordinary claims.

For instance, the tale of Mongol riches is real and some could have been at Khara-khoto. After years of campaigns conquering peoples from the Caspian Sea to the Pacific Ocean, the Mongols brought back untold wealth, as well as the finest craftsmen. French artisan Guillaume Boucher designed the Silver Tree for the Khan's palace in the capital of Kharakorum. Described in his account of his thirteenth century journey to the East, William of Rubruck wrote:

> At the entrance to this palace, seeing it would have been unseemly to put skins of milk and other drinks there, Master William of Paris has made for him a large silver tree, at the foot of which are four silver lions each having a pipe and all belching forth white mares milk. Inside the trunk four pipes lead up to the top of the tree and the ends of the pipes are bent downwards and over each of them is a gilded serpent, the tail of which twines round the trunk of the tree. One of these pipes pours out wine, another caracosmos [airag], that is the refined milk of mares, another boal, which is a honey drink, and another rice mead, which is called terracina. Each of these has its silver basin ready to receive it at the foot of the tree between the other four pipes. At the very top he fashioned an angel holding a trumpet; underneath the tree he made a crypt in which a man can be secreted, and a pipe goes up to the angel through the middle of the heart of the tree. At first he had made bellows but they did not give enough wind. Outside the palace there is a chamber in which the drinks are stored, and servants stand there ready to pour them out when they hear the angel sounding the trumpet. The tree has branches, leaves and fruit of silver. And so when the drinks are getting low the chief butler calls out to the angel to sound his trumpet. Then, hearing this, the man who is hidden in the crypt blows the pipe going up to the angel with all his strength, and the angel, placing the trumpet to his mouth, sounds it very loudly. When the servants in the chamber hear this each one of them pours out his drink into its proper pipe, and the pipes pour them out from above and below into the basins prepared for this, and then the cup-bearers draw the drinks and carry them round the palace to the men and women.

The journey of William of Rubruck to the eastern parts of the world, 1253-55 page 208

Evidence of the great wealth of Karakhorum, the capital of the Mongol Empire, still exists today. The enormous city walls stand battered by time, but still visible. Remnants of the green-glazed tiles that once adorned the roofs are present as well as paved streets and buildings constructed of brick and adobe. One can only imagine their wealth after the conquest of the Song Dynasty and creating the Yuan dynasty. Proclaiming himself Emperor in 1271, Kublai Khan moved his capital first to Shangdu (Xanadu) and then Dadu (Khanbaliq), near where Beijing stands today.

After the Chinese Ming displaced Mongol Yuan rule in China in 1368, it would not be a large stretch of the imagination for Mongolian general Buyan Temurn to be transporting riches away to the Mongol controlled territory of the Northern Yuan. Slowed by the desert sands and treasures weighing down a long procession of pack animals, the good general would seek refuge in a city Chinggis Khan conquered over 150 years earlier. Did the Ming forces divert the Ejin River from its normal course, did they merely plug up a nearby canal feeding the cities' water supply, or did the river simply dry up on its own? Did the surrounded forces escape into the desert, did they all fight to the end, or did they survive as Ming prisoners? Hopefully, archaeological and geological information can answer some of the questions. I believe we need to wait until we know if the diversion of the river was a natural phenomenon or not, or whether the bones of the warriors are unearthed before I agree on the veracity of any version of this tale of Buyan Temurn and Khara-Khoto. There needs to be some verifiable information available to answer hard questions because fantastic statements require fantastic evidence or proofs to substantiate them.

On the Trail of Ancient Man by Roy Chapman Andrews in 1922 brought tales of the giant Mongolian Death worm whose touch brings a quick death after excruciating pain. The tale also mentions the two to five-foot-long worm can also kill at a distance with an electrical charge or spitting venom. I cannot spot the kernel of truth in this tale, maybe the creation of another machination to explain why perfectly healthy people die in the desert. I will accept the tale without making any moral judgement; however, without proof I do not have to believe it is real. On the other hand, if I am ever in Mongolia and the sand starts to stir and some red worm pops its head up, I will control my urge to pet it.

One of the reasons to analyze the tales of the Great Uighur Empire is to bring some truth to the imaginative tales espoused by my great-grandfather, James Churchward, in his books and used by others to support nefarious agendas. One such example is a group once led by the late Empress of Mu. Based on her interpretation as the hereditary ruler of Mu, her sovereignty included all of the Americas and superseded the authority of the United States government and/or state and local governments. For so many dollars, anyone could become a citizen of her Washitaw nation. Washitaw 'citizenship' permitted its citizens to ignore the requirements of driver's licenses and taxes. Laugh as you may at this absurdity, but the people paying money believed they had the right to ignore the IRS and income taxes. Needless to say, the IRS always gets its money. The assertion James Churchward's books validates their claims is absolutely bogus. The following passage from James' 1931 book, *Children of Mu* contradicts their contention:

> As is shown by various documents, Atlantis had a colored population in the south. I have never come across any documents showing that any Negroes were known in Central and North America. Being in Atlantis and none being in Central and North America, the question was: how did they get into Atlantis? Subsequently the Tibetian map answered the question—they came through the Amazonian Sea, therefore, never touched Central or North America.
> *Children of Mu*, page 101

While I hold no ill will towards the followers of the late Empress Mu, my concern is for those duped and subsequently suffering criminal prosecution. While I have no control over the use of my great-grandfather's theories, I do have the right to point out the errors and perhaps prevent someone unwittingly stumbling into a compromising situation.

When I undertook my research, I wanted to answer the questions I received over the years and gain a greater understanding of my great-grandfather and his life. Also, to 'lift the veil' on his pseudo-history/archaeology and to figure out the underlying reasons his books are still in print and attracting new followers after ninety years. There is no implied moral compass automatically relegating certain labels on his works (or followers) in my mind; they are simply words from a time when many more people believed in the possibility of fantastic things because they did not know any better. With the advancement of science over the past nine decades and the improvements in education, one would think these outdated and rejected theories would go by the wayside.

Chapter 2: James Churchward's Great Uighur Empire

According to census documents, James Churchward was born in Bridestowe, Devonshire, England on February 28, 1851, the fifth child with four brothers and four sisters. Although many biographies repeat the claim he was educated at Oxford and Sandhurst Military College, queries to these institutions have yielded no evidence to substantiate these claims. Census documents indicate James was employed as a Bank Clerk in London in 1871 and a marriage license from that year indicates his marriage to Mary Julia Stephenson in December. Other documentation shows my grandfather, Alexander James Churchward was born in Ceylon (now Sri Lanka) in September 1872. Newspaper accounts and other records place James as the owner/operator of tea plantations in Sri Lanka during the 1870s. From family correspondence, I learned James lost his tea plantations and set out across the Pacific in 1880, eventually ending up the United States. From his unpublished biography, he was known in the 1880s in New York and discussed Theosophy and other subjects with Augustus LePlongeon and others in Sunday afternoon tea sessions. James wrote two travel brochures for the railroads in the 1890s, submitted articles in hunting and fishing magazines and was awarded seven US patents. After the turn of the century, James was awarded many more patents and eventually sued a major Steel manufacturer for a million dollars for infringing on his patent for nickel chromium vanadium steel used in armor plating on US warships. He eventually was awarded a smaller sum and moved from New York to a seven-acre estate in Lakeville, Connecticut. James also contributed illustrations to his brother Albert's books on Freemasonry.

Newspaper accounts of James pronouncements on the lost continent of Mu first appeared in 1924. W.E. Rudge published James' first book on his Mu theories in 1926 entitled, *The Lost Continent of Mu Motherland of Men* where he began his explanation in detail. He states the story started when he served in India as a Bengal Lancer during the 1870s; as part of his duties supporting famine relief, he visited a nearby temple and became acquainted with the resident Rishi. After their friendship developed, the Rishi confided in him, only he and his brother were the remaining members of the ancient Naacal Brotherhood. This Brotherhood had maintained and protected the ancient knowledge and wisdom of the now sunken Pacific Ocean continent of Mu for millennia. The Rishi taught James the meaning behind the symbols on the temple walls and eventually brought out ancient clay tablets to examine with James. These were a partial set of the Naacal Tablets, the repository of knowledge and wisdom of the Naacal Brotherhood. The tablets told the story of Mu, the birthplace of mankind, the proverbial "Garden of Eden." Dating back two-hundred thousand years, Mu reached a higher level of civilization than what he experienced in the early 20th century. All the peoples lived peacefully and enjoyed free education, plentiful food, and special powers over the forces of nature. He wrote the adventuresome people of Mu, he called them the Maya, went forth from Mu in ancient times to colonize the world. Those departing from the west formed the Uighur Empire starting in Northern Asia, and the Naga Empire in southern Asia. Those sailing east colonized the Americas, Europe, Atlantis and Africa. Some 12,000 to 14,000 years ago, the great Magnetic Cataclysm, (also known as the Biblical Flood,) destroyed the continents of Mu and Atlantis in a single day and sunk them beneath the waves. At the same time of the destruction of Mu, the eastern half of the Uighur Empire was destroyed in a north running wave of water and the mountains were thrust up into the formerly flat surfaced spherical earth.

To be fair and complete, certain inconvenient facts undermine James Churchward's pronouncements on the lost continent of Mu. There is no evidence to suggest James was in the Bengal Lancers of the British Army in the 1870s; however, there are records placing him in Sri Lanka (Ceylon) in the 1870s as the owner and operator of tea plantations. The correspondence between my great-grandmother and one of James' brothers after she heard one of James' broadcasts on WNYC in the 1920s seals that debate. She wrote, "he is no more a colonel than you or I." Other inconvenient facts include he was the only one to have seen the Naacal tablets relating the remarkable story of Mu, he took no notes or pictures of these spectacular artifacts, and he waited over forty-five years to tell anyone about his amazing discovery. He could have been the talk of the town and he had a weekly audience in the 1890s to make it happen. This by no means is a complete disclosure; however, it does provide the reader a more complete picture and understanding of James Churchward's credentials to author books on Mu.

James devotes a complete chapter to the Great Uighur Empire in the 1931 *Children of Mu*, long passages in both versions of the *Lost Continent of Mu* and makes frequent mentions throughout the rest of his material. His writings state the Uighurs controlled the largest empire known to history, essentially most of Asia and all of Europe. They were the Aryans, bringing civilization from Mu through their western migration/colonization of the planet. James also references ancient records to show the antiquity of the Great Uighur Empire. Placed throughout his works are references to and interpretations of artifacts and symbols he attributed to the Uighur. He dates these to before the destructive north running wave wiped out the eastern half of their empire. Unfortunately, James' fable descends further into racial stereotypes and denigrates entire peoples. The following paragraphs examine James' theories of the Great Uighur Empire. Every attempt has been undertaken to research the source material for these theories. I have had an open invitation on my website for over ten years requesting corroborative data. Some Turkish readers have attempted to provide information; however, it always appears to circle back to James' writings. Appendices have been included to provide every mention of 'Uighur' in James' published works to supplement the narrative.

In James' theories, the Uighur Empire was "the principal colonial empire belonging to Mu before the great 'Biblical' flood destroyed its eastern half." The empire stretched "from the Pacific Ocean across Central Asia and into Eastern Europe from the Caspian Sea on [...] Eventually the Uighurs extended themselves into Europe around the western and northern shores of the Caspian Sea [...] from there they continued in through Central Europe to its western boundary, Ireland." The northern boundary was far into Siberia and the southern border was through 'Cochin China,' Burma, India, and Persia, "before the Himalayas and other Asiatic mountains were raised."

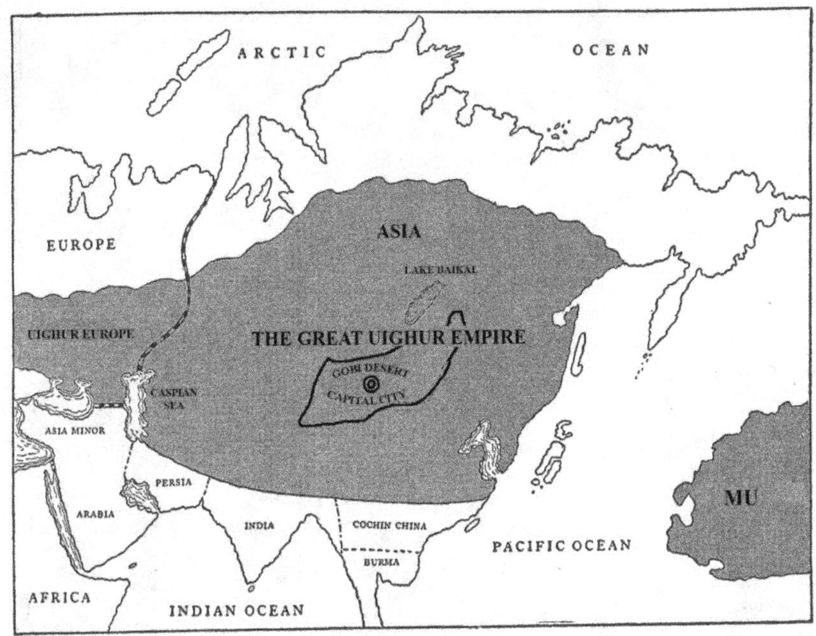

Figure 8: James' Map of the Great Uighur Empire from *Lost Continent of Mu Motherland of Men*

James states, "the history of the Uighurs is the history of the Aryans" and "forefathers of all the Aryan races." His quoted description of the Uighurs from a Chinese record dated to 500 B.C. relates:

> "The Uighurs were all of a light complexion, milk-white skins, with varying color of eyes and hair. In the north blue eyes and light hair predominated. In the south were found those with dark hair and dark eyes."
> *Children of Mu*, page 217

The Great Uighur Empire during the Tertiary Era.

Figure 9: The Great Uighur Empire during the Tertiary Period, *Children of Mu*

James also remarks not all white people are Aryans, some of them followed different routes and are not descended from the Uighur. His 'real' Aryans knew "astrology, mining, textile industries, mathematics, agriculture, writing, reading, medicine, etc." They were "experts in decorative art on silk, metal, and wood and made statues of gold, silver, bronze and clay; and this was before the history of Egypt commenced." Were one to replace astronomy with astrology, these accomplishments could be associated with the historical Idiqut State described in Part 1 (except the part about Egypt.)

As far as dating the Great Uighur Empire, James states "The Uighurs formed chains of settlements across the central parts of Europe back in *Tertiary Times*." This provides a contradiction in James' writings since he wrote the Mu civilization was only 200,000 years old and the Tertiary Period lasted from 65,000,000 years ago to 2,500,000 years ago. Since the main premise of the story of the 'lost continent of Mu' insists all humans originated from Mu, the establishment of Uighur settlements appears to be millions of years before Mu had a civilization. Ignoring the inconsistency, it obviously took many years for the Uighurs to develop their empire and create the conditions to permit them accommodation of the higher aspects of Mu civilization. James quotes the Naacal writings he encountered in a 'Tibetian' monastery to say:

> "The Naacals, 70,000 years ago, brought to the Uighur capital cities copies of the Sacred Inspired Writings of the Motherland."
> *Children of Mu*, page 217

Additionally, James informs us his Great Uighur Empire gained its height around 17,000 years ago. These dates provide a fantastic, unsubstantiated timeline. As described in Part 1, current archaeological evidence shows the length of human habitation in Inner Asia much less than the speculation of millions of years or 70,000 years. We might extend the time back to 125,000 B.P were we to include the Neanderthal and/or Denisovans. Another presumption of James' theories contends the then-recent discoveries of Neanderthal, Piltdown and Heildelberg man were human; "remains were those of idiots and degenerates is obvious from the abnormal shapes of their skulls." He further states they were "outcasts from civilized society." If so, where are the remains of the 'civilized society' casting them out?

Unfortunately for James' theories, current archaeological evidence cited in Part 1 shows the use of stone tools and habitations consisting of small settlements; higher technology and the capital cities have remained hidden. One might point to his 'magnetic cataclysm destroying the eastern half of the Uighur Empire' as one reason for the lack of evidence, however that excuse holds no water since the remains of the ancient, sedentary peoples living there somehow survived. If there were great cities, something of their accomplishments would survive if the remains of a 'less-civilized' people living in shelters made of animal bone and hides withstood the adversity of time and his cataclysm. A subsequent discussion provides even another reason to reject these earlier dates.

Proof of the north running destructive wave is also included with the description of the Great Uighur Empire. The debris, consisting of boulders, gravel and sand, covering the 'ancient' city of Khara-Khoto was "the work of water as acknowledged by all geologists throughout the world." James ties this 'flood' to the north running wave of the Last Magnetic Cataclysm, the Biblical 'Flood.'

James also relates his participation in a geological investigation north of Lake Baikal to the mouth of the Lena River on the Arctic Ocean. All along the way the signs of this catastrophe, including the entire region of Siberia, became evident. James insists the wave was ice-free due to what they found on Llakoff's Island, just off the mouth of the Lena River in the Arctic Ocean. According to James, the expedition found entire islands made from "bones and tusks of mammoths and other forest animals which had been swept up from the Mongolian and Siberian plains by the flood and carried to this, their final resting place." His conclusion yielded, "the presence of these bones confirms the flood was ice-free; otherwise, the ice would have crushed the bones to a pulp."

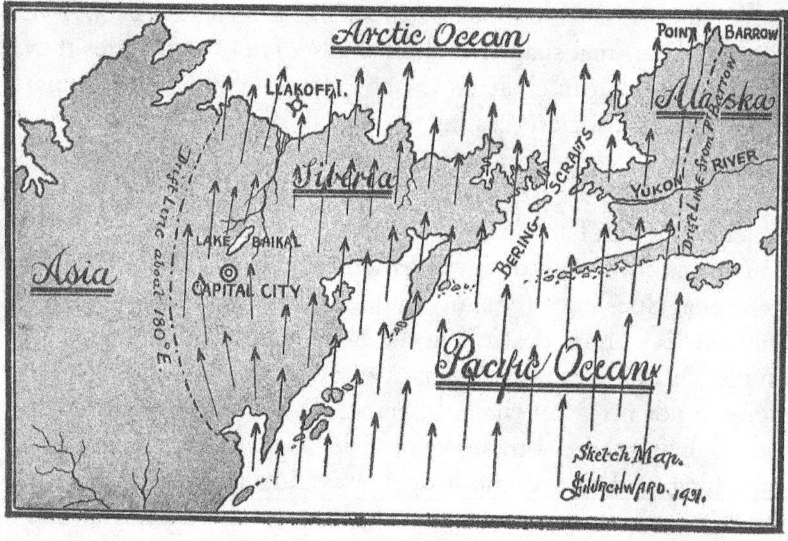

Figure 10: Illustration of the path of the north running wave, *Children of Mu*

Llakoff's Island is actually the Lyakhovsky Islands, also spelled Liakhov in Jules Verne's books, *Waif of the Cynthia* (1885) and *César Cascabel* (1890.) It is true the islands appear to be made of the bones of ancient animals. Since the discovery of the islands, excavations have pulled tons of their bones from their sands and been shipped around the world. While this fact does not prove the north running wave theory during the Biblical flood, perhaps the absence of any record of human remains on these islands will disassociate the theory with the Great Uighur Empire. In the 1927 *Books of the Golden Age*, James asserts "thousands of millions of humans" inhabited Asia prior to the Great Magnetic Cataclysm. One might expect the bones retrieved from these islands would also include some from the former human population as well. Another point to ponder, James implies the presence of the mammoth was concurrent with the advanced Uighur Empire, since there are/were entire islands made of their bones. If so, how did the billions of people deal with large herds of these enormous herbivores? Since there were no mountains yet, mammoth stampedes must have posed a great danger to the public as they ranged across the plains.

James includes artifacts and symbols he attributes to the ancient Uighur throughout his works. One example is the "scepter carried by a monarch of the Uighurs" displayed in the 1926 *Lost Continent of Mu Motherland of Men* on page 109.

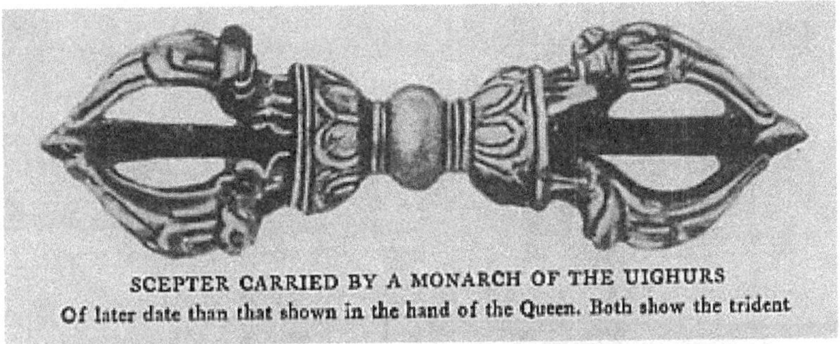
SCEPTER CARRIED BY A MONARCH OF THE UIGHURS
Of later date than that shown in the hand of the Queen. Both show the trident

Figure 11: "Scepter carried by a monarch of the Uighur Of later date than that shown in the hand of the Queen. Both show the trident" or "A golden Scepter of one of the ancient kings found in the secret tomb."

The 'scepter' is actually a religious ritual item, a Vajra (Tibetan: dorje.) The Sanskrit meaning of Vajra is both thunderbolt and diamond. In the Hindu tradition, is it is the weapon of the god Indra. In Vajrayana Buddhism, it represents the 'thunderbolt' experience of Buddhist enlightenment and the indestructability of the achievement. The symbol is shown in the hand of an 'Uighur Queen' on page 108. James interprets the three points on the end of her Vajra to show a "trident – three points – the Motherland's symbol." The three points on her crown show the escutcheon of a colonial empire, the large sun symbol painted behind them represents Mu and the smaller circular figure represents the Uighur Empire. The image is purportedly from the Khara-Khoto expedition by the Russian explorer P.K. Kozlov.

With mention of P.K. Kozlov and Khara-Khoto, the need arises to address a clipping from one of James' scrapbooks (and transcribed in Appendix 8.)

Originally published as "In the Secret Tomb of Earth's Oldest Kings" by the America Weekly in 1924 (San Antonio Light 1924-09-07 p.2,) the article is an example of yellow journalism, when sensational stories sold newspapers. In the scrapbook version, the previous title does not appear and replacing it is "Khara Khota Kosloff." Much information contained in James' discussion of the Great Uighur Empire, including the two previously mentioned images, is contained in the article. Of course, James provides a special spin in his version.

Loaned from the Collection of the American Weekly Section of the New York Sunday American
AN UIGHUR QUEEN AND HER CONSORT

Figure 12: "An Uighur Queen and Her Consort" or "Paintings upon silk, as fresh to-day almost as they were when they were put away 8,000 years

ago, and which reveal the sources from which China, India, and Persia copied the pictures and statues of their various Gods and Goddesses'

James' description of the Uighur as "[...] light complexion, milk-white skins, [...]" contained in an unnamed Chinese record is a slight modification to the article's declaration:

> "Somewhere from the south of Mongolia, from the present day province of Alashan of China, rose this white and strong nation. The origin of the Uighurs is problematic. But it is known that they ruled all the border lands of China, India and Mongolia, spread gradually northward, and eventually controlled all the more or less advanced nomadic tribes.
> The greatest power of the Uighurs extended from 6000 B.C. till the rise of the new Chinese, Indian, and Persian empires. The Chinese annals of 500 B.C. describe them as being a light-haired and blue-eyed people."

This portion of the article is suspiciously similar to the following passage on page 51 of the 1914 *Unknown Mongolia* by Douglas Carruthers:

> "[...] Somewhere from the far south of Mongolia, perhaps from the borders of China - from the present-day provinces of Shensi and Kansu - came a wandering people, the Uigurs. The origin of the Uigurs is problematic, but as far back as this it can be traced with fair certainty. [...] The greatest power of the Uigurs (according to Professor Adrianoff of Minnusinsk) 'extended from the fourth to the eight century, when they exercised considerable political ascendency in these districts. The Chinese annals described them as being a light-haired and blue-eyed people. They were probably, at this period, of a very mixed race, showing great variation in type, especially as regards the protraction of the eye-lid. In the ancient Uigurs we have the origin of the Turkish race, who, later on, overflowed all Central Asia and made an empire on the shore of the Bosphorus. The history of the Uigurs and the migrations of the Turki tribes are outside our story; it is only the influence these races had upon the people of the Yenisei region that affects us."

The historical documents covered in Part 1 support Carruther's brief description of the Uighur. Documents composed in Persian, Byzantine and the Chinese language describe the Gok-Turk and Uighur and their activities in the fourth through eighth centuries CE. Obvious to the most casual observer, the yellow journalist composing the article decided to create mysterious circumstances and replace the original dates with an unsubstantiated figure of 6,000 BC. James Churchward added a few years to place the date of the height of the Uighur Empire to 17,000 years ago to allow their presence prior to his Great Magnetic Cataclysm.

James asserts the location of the Uighur capital as Khara-Khoto (forgiving his misspelling.) The article recounts Khara-Khoto as the capital of Chinggis Khan and Kublai Khan. As we have seen, the Uighur and Great Khan's capitals lay further north in the Orkhon Valley, over 350 miles away. Kublai's capital was close to today's Beijing, over 800 miles to the southeast. In reality, Khara-Khoto was a thriving center of trade in the Tangut Empire (Xi Xia), the Tangut being a people practicing Mahayana / Vajrayana Buddhism.

Both James and the article agree Kozlov dug fifty feet under Khara-Khoto to uncover precious relics, except if you read James' 1927 *Books of the Golden Age.* In that retelling, an explorer named McClelland dug down the 40 to 50 feet through the boulders, gravel and sand in 1906 to find the Capital City of the Uighurs. Kozlov first visited the relatively undisturbed site in April of 1908.

In the article, at the bottom of the excavation lay the graves of the Seven Kings of Tartary with their all their riches. According to the article, they represented the kings of the Uighur Empire from 8,000 to 6,000 BCE. Also provided is the admonition to the explorers, "[...] the condition that he should not take away the dead, or anything that belonged to them, but see and copy everything he wished, and cover again the place with sand." James' discussion of the "wonderful treasures" related the stipulation placed on Kozlov, as "he was only allowed to take pictures and not allowed to disturb or take anything away." This necessitated James' use of the photos from the American Weekly article, since Kozlov supposedly left everything there. In real life, Kozlov brought back many splendid treasures from the ruins of Khara-Khoto to Saint Petersburg, Russia; the artifacts are on display in the Hermitage Museum and include 2,000 books written in the Tangut language.

While described as "photos," the images James included and interpreted were two drawings from the six in the article. It should be pointed out the article's caption to James' 'Uighur Queen and Her Consort' image read "Paintings upon silk, as fresh to-day almost as they were when they were put away 8,000 years ago, and which reveal the sources from which China, India, and Persia copied the pictures and statues of their various Gods and Goddesses." The caption on the image of the Vajra read "A golden Scepter of one of the ancient kings found in the secret tomb."

Another of the images from the article is used as the frontispiece for his 1933 book, *Sacred Symbols of Mu* symbolizing "The First Man, Dual Principle" with the additional attribution "Courtesy of P. K. Kosloff. Over 20,000 years old. From the ancient Uighur Capital, beneath Karakhota, Gobi Desert." The caption in the article reads: "A curious two-headed figure found in the lap of one of the mummies and which was evidently the object of great holiness." A quick internet search ("Double Headed Buddha") provides the real answer; the statue is part of the Hermitage Museum collection in Saint Petersburg, Russia. The description identifies the statue: "Double Headed Buddha. The Mongol period of Khara-Khoto, Mongolia. (1227-end of the 14th century). Clay, straw, traces of painting and gilding." A further description provides:

> This story was told to a Chinese pilgrim during one of his long wanderings in the north: once upon a time, there were two men, both devoted to the teachings of Buddha. Each of them dreamed an image of the Buddha, but they were too poor to pay for two sculptures, so they asked an artist to make them only one. Buddha himself, in an act of kindness, divided the image in two. Kindness, or compassion, is an important teaching of Buddhism.
> This clay statue was found in the stupa uncovered by Kozlov in 1909. The statue is made from the simple materials of earth and straw, but the artist has given the

Buddha a smile and a gentle tilt to the head, and added colour and gold to the two faces to emphasise Buddha's compassionate nature.

Adding up the knowledge that these are images of relics from an ancient Buddhist city (Khara-Khoto,) combined with the recognizable Buddhist iconography, James' interpretation of the discoveries as 20,000 year old Uighur Empire artifacts indicates either a tall tale or ignorance of Buddhist symbolism (or both.)

Another statue potentially attributed to James' Great Uighur Empire is contained in the 1931 *Children of Mu.* Captioned as "One of the two oldest bronzes in the world – a symbolic figure of Mu as the mistress and ruler of the whole earth. It was made in either Mu or in the Uighur Capital City over 20,000 years ago." Again, the distinct Buddhist iconography and the known use of bronze indicate a different interpretation. The excavations at Mohenjo-daro in Pakistan have yielded the earliest example of bronze statues dating from 2500 BCE from the Harappan civilization of the Indus Valley. While there may be earlier examples of bronze statues found in the future, none will bridge the gap of 15,500 years to legitimize James Churchward's description.

Figure 13: "The First Man, Dual Principle" or "A Curious Two-Headed Figure Found in the Lap of One of the Mummies and Which was Evidently the Object of Great Holiness."

As previously stated, some of the material from the article is repeated word-for-word in James' accounts. For instance, in the article is this passage:

> "The Uighurs, as the race was called, reached a high degree of culture: they knew astrology, mining, textile industry, architecture, mathematics, agriculture, writing and reading, medicine and Magianism. They had excellent training in decorative arts on silk, metal, and wood, and they made statues of gold and silver and wood, clay and bronze."

Courtesy of George N. Leiper

One of the two oldest known bronzes in the world—a symbolical figure of Mu as the mistress and ruler of the whole earth. It was made in either Mu or in the Uighur Capital City over 20,000 years ago.

Figure 14: One of the two oldest bronzes in the world – a symbolic figure of Mu as the mistress and ruler of the whole earth. It was made in either Mu or in the Uighur Capital City over 20,000 years ago.

James' description of the Uighur, previously quoted (see page 58,) replaces 'Magianism' with 'etc.' and instead of 'excellent training,' James declared they were experts. Additionally, James repeated almost the same admonition concerning the relics removed from Khara-Khoto and both agree on the description of the Gobi Desert as a "[...] cultivated land of fertile fields, forests, lakes and rivers." Both narratives continue with the following:

> "with magnificently constructed roads and highways connecting the various cities and towns with each other. These were well built cities, huge temples and public institutions, elaborate private houses and palaces of the rulers."

James' further use of material from the article follow in a later portion, however, the article and James' accounts ignore

Occam's Razor; rather than some fantastic explanation and interpretation of the relics found by Kozlov, the historic record, although less fantastic, provides a reasonable explanation. As opposed to the dating and analysis of the actual relics discovered in Khara-khoto, James' and the yellow journalist's fantastic accounts rely on legends, hearsay, and the uninformed interpretation of a few drawings to create their tale of a mythical ancient Asian civilization. As a final point, Kozlov's diaries of his expeditions do not match the wondrous accounts revealed in the article or in James' texts.

James references the "Book of Manu," an "ancient Hindu book" with regards to his Great Uighur Empire. In the 1931 *Children of Mu*, he asserts a passage in the aforementioned tome includes "The Uighurs had a settlement on the northern and eastern shores of the Caspian Sea."

He relates this to the migration of the Uighur in the Pleistocene (2,588,00 – 11,700 YBP) as described by Max Mueller and after the mountains were raised.

The Book of Manu is more commonly known as the Laws of Manu or Manava Dharma Sastra and it is indeed an ancient Hindu book, but the contents are not normally accepted as a reliable historical treatise. A "revealed" scripture of twelve chapters, the 2684 verses describe the social, domestic and religious norms of life in first and second century BCE India. It is one of the supplemental portions of Vedic literature and delineates the caste system imposed by the Brahmins. The work has been translated into English and the version by George Buhler from 1886 is available on sacredtexts.com. While the text does speak of the subjugation of women and the almost reverential attitude towards the Brahmins, it is not a history book. Looking for the other mentions of the same text in James' works, it is mentioned in the 1926 *Lost Continent of Mu Motherland of Men*. Of the three mentions of the Manava Dharma Sastra, two are found to be reworded passages from Augustus LePlongeon's 1896 *Queen Moo and the Egyptian Sphinx*. The other mention reads: "Manava Dharma Sastra, a Hindi book, refers to the Serpent as the Creator." The only mention of serpent I was able to discover was in the tenth chapter and requires penance if, after killing a serpent or other creature, the twice born man is unable to atone by the giving of gifts.

'*China* by E.H. Parker' is another reference James uses in his discussion of his Great Uighur Empire. The complete title of the 1901 volume is *China, Her History, Diplomacy, and Commerce: From the Earliest Times to the Present Day* by Edward Harper Parker. James refers to and presents the information on the table from page 17 as referenced; however, as in other cases, he presents the data and then maligns the source to establish the primacy of his pronouncements. Below is the portion of the table James' cited from page 17 of Parker's *China […]*:

Name of Dynasty	Number of Rulers	Duration of Dynasty
"Five Monarchs"	Nine	2852-2206 B.C
Hia	Eighteen	2205-1767 B.C
Shang	Twenty-eight	1766-1122 B.C
Chow	Ten	1121-828 B.C.
Chow	Twenty-five	827-225 B.C.

James follows up with a textual summary of the information in the fourth/last column.

EARLY CHINESE DYNASTIES.

Name of Dynasty.	Number of Rulers.	Duration of Dynasty.	Remarks.
"Five Monarchs"	Nine	2852–2206	Altogether mythical.
Hia	Eighteen	2205–1767	Legendary and largely mythical.
Shang	Twenty-eight	1766–1122	Chiefly legendary.
Chou	Ten	1122–828	Semi-historical kings.
,,	Twenty-five	827–255	Recognised as historical by Sz-ma Ts'ien.

Figure 15: *China, Her History, Diplomacy, and Commerce: From the Earliest Times to the Present Day*; E.H. Parker; 1910; page 17

Subsequently, James begins his diatribe:

"From the foregoing one must infer that Parker believes only what he sees and nothing that he hears. It would appear that it matters not how true a legend may be, it is a myth unless he sees writings which he can believe in. It has been one of my hobbies to trace myths back to see what they come out of. Ninety times out of a hundred I have found that the myth has its origin in a tradition or legend. The tradition or legend has been so garbled that it has become a perfect myth. It should be remembered that there is no smoke without a fire. I do not doubt for a minute that in many cases what Parker calls myths are really legends slightly garbled. They are traditions only to the people, for behind them in the old Tao temples are to be found written records of the various phenomena.

Parker gives a good and very exhaustive history of China from about 200 B.C. down to present time. He shows the rise and fall of the various Mongol tribes and nations. He is, however, absolutely wrong about the Japanese; and, being wrong about them, other assertions of his are left open to doubt. From his style of writing he would be one to put poor old Marco Polo in prison because he did not bring back a big-horn sheep to show. How Parker accounts for the Gobi ruins and other great prehistoric ruins, I do not know. Apparently, such things mean nothing to him."
Children of Mu, page 226

This technique is very similar to the opening passage he uses to introduce the information about the Great Uighur Empire in the 1926 *Lost Continent of Mu Motherland of Men* on page 106.

"I think the Uighur records will be all that is necessary to convince the most skeptical mind that it is clearly proven by symbols alone that Mu was the motherland of man; but, as an old Hindu saying goes:
"It is easier to snatch a pearl from the teeth of a crocodile, or to twist an angry, venomous serpent around one's head like a garland of flowers, without incurring danger, than to make an Ignorant or an obstinate person change his mind."

The discussion of James' reproduction and interpretation of 'Uighur' symbols presented next clearly indicates there are no 'Uighur records' to substantiate his theory of the lost civilization of Mu. This diatribe is simply a device to dismiss contrary information and bring the reader 'into the fold' by revealing his supposedly hidden knowledge. Likewise, James' ad hominem attack on E.H. Parker and his description of early Chinese dynasties permits the rejection of Parker's account of Chinese history. Edward Harper Parker studied the Chinese language, served at the British consulates of Wenchow, Fusan, and Shanghai in China and travelled extensively throughout Asia and Oceania. Parker also wrote some fifteen works on Chinese life and history. James' descriptions of his travels do not mention any time spent in China, nor do his academic credentials indicate a special study of China or her history. James' repudiation of Parker to support his Great Uighur Empire theory, in part, relies on the dubious contents of a yellow journalism article. James maliciously dismisses the one real expert he includes in the discussion of his theory.

James provides his interpretations of symbols he identifies as 'Uighur' in his demonstrations linking all cultures and civilizations back to Mu. From his chapter on the Cliff-Dwellers in the 1926 *Lost Continent of Mu Motherland of Men*, he attributes two symbols in his "Symbols Found Among the Cliff-Dwellers' Writings" illustration with the Uighur Maya.

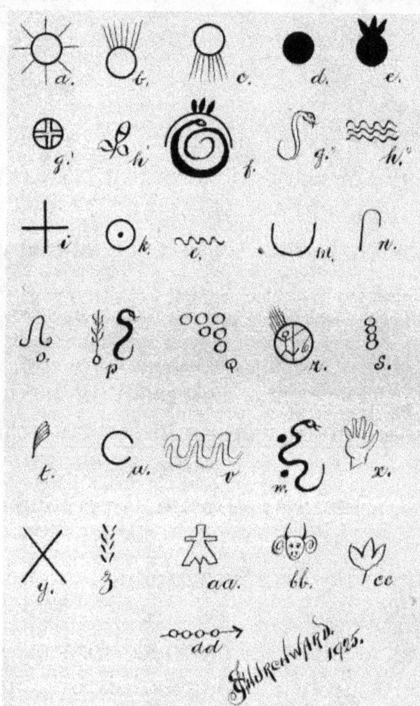

Figure 16: Symbols Found Among the Cliff Dwellers' Writings; *Lost Continent of Mu Motherland of Men*

From page 177:
"R. This is an Uighur-Maya religious symbol.
S. This is the Uighur hieratic letter h."

James brings the Uighur-Maya to Nevada in his explanation of the petroglyphs discovered in Gold Gulch, Beatty.

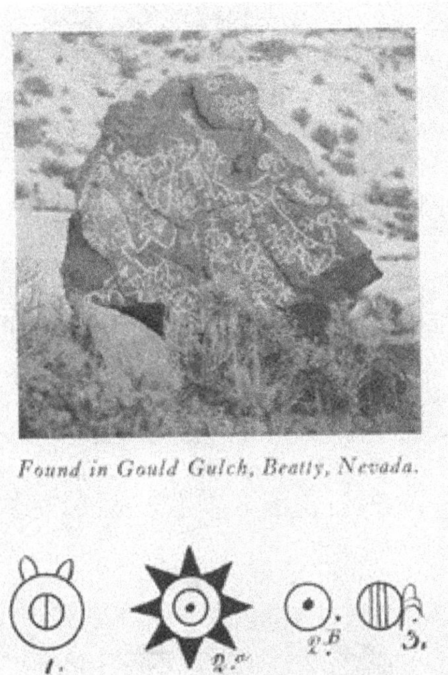

Figure 17: (Symbols) Found in Gould Gulch, Beatty, Nevada

James interpretation of the three symbols from page 182 reads:

1. reads, chi-pe-zi, which, translated, means "A mouth opened, fires came forth with vapors, the land gave way and went down."
2a. This is the escutcheon of the Empire of the Sun, the land of Mu. A sun with eight rays. Instead of the center being a symbol reading, "The Empire of-," this has in its place: 2b, "Ahau, the King, the Great King, the Great Ruler."

Freely read, the writings on this face say: "A mouth opened, volcanic fires and vapors came forth, the land gave

> way, and Mu, the Great Ruler, the Empire of the Sun, sank into that abyss of fire."
>
> On the left arm of the figure, the first symbol is (3) the-the-ha, which, translated, reads: "Toward water, or in the direction of water."

Further quoting James, on the petroglyphs, "The characters on this picture are all Uighur-Maya. These people may have been Mongols." Of course, this supports James' declaration in his chapter on Niven's Mexican Cities, where he states on page 220, "Eventually, however, the northern hordes of Mongols overran and conquered the whole of Mexico and Central America."

In the 1931 *Children of Mu*, James schools the reader on the representation of Uighur numbers as follows:

> "The Uighurs, generally, used a bar or line to express their numerals but quite often reverted to the Naga when inscribing the Mysterious Writing. At times, however, they expressed the Mysterious Writing with their popular form of glyphs. (Figs. 1, 2 and 3.) Sometimes these lines were drawn horizontally, sometimes vertically, apparently dependent on the form of space available. (Figs. 4 and 5.) " *Children of Mu* page 57

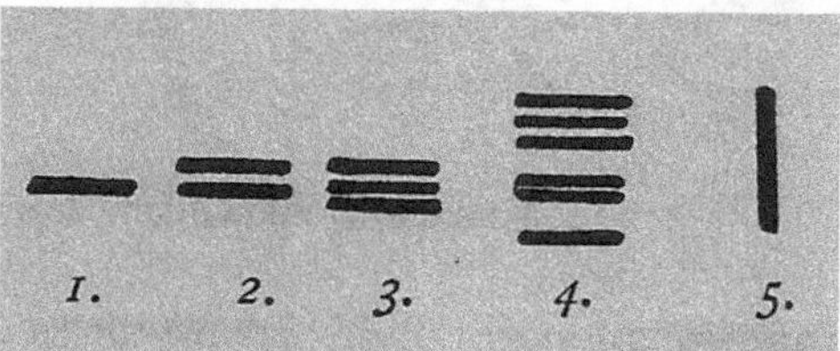

Figure 18: "Mysterious Writing"; *Children of Mu*

Another of James' examples of Uighur writing decorates the Cara or Kara Inscription in northeastern Brazil. Although James attributes most of the characters to the ancient Carians, he did find some written in Uighur.

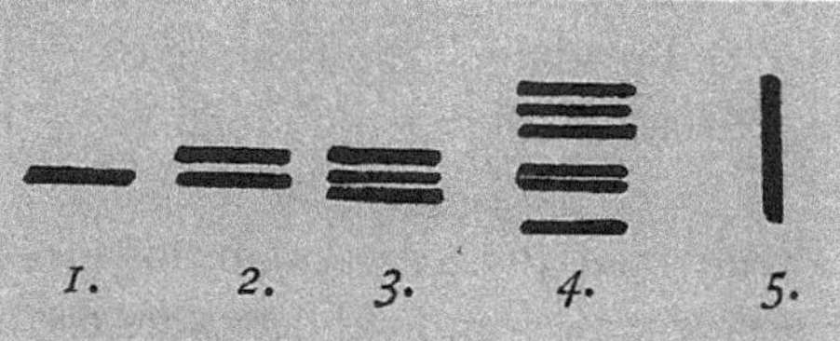

Figure 19: "Uighur Numerals"

> "A universal symbol as before stated (Fig. 1.). The Northern or Uighur form of symbol for writing the numeral one (Fig. 2.). Numeral 2 (Fig. 3.). Numeral 3 (Fig. 4.). Numeral 3 is specialized by not having one end closed."; *Children of Mu*

Uighur writing also adorns the "Teotihuacan pyramid" (page 60) and "Most of the Tao te King is made up of extracts from the Uighur copy of the Sacred Inspired Writings of Mu" (page 61.) James' finds Uighur writing among the now-discredited 'stone tablets' discovered by William Niven in the valley of Mexico in the early 19th century. These are just some examples and the contents of the 1932 *Sacred Symbols of Mu* have yet to enter the discussion. Further mentions and interpretations of symbols from James' writings provide no path to the truth and are left to the reader to explore at their leisure (see Appendices.) James' list of Uighur cultural achievements includes reading and writing. Yet, never a sample of ancient Uighur writing graces the pages of his books, only individual symbols he alone can translate or interpret. If James' Uighur travelled widely (as implied by the myriad of locations where 'Uighur' writing appeared,) should we find not only 'Uighur' symbols but also short historical or religious works carved in stone and/or other evidence of their presence?

The real Old Uyghur alphabet, derived from the same Sogdian characters carved into stone on the Orkhon Inscriptions, lasted until the 18th century and serves as parent to the Mongol and Manchu alphabets. The Old Uyghur alphabet written vertically in columns and read from left to right should not be confused or associated with the symbols identified by James as 'Uighur.'

A final point where James' writings on the Uighur and the article "In the Secret Tomb of Earth's Oldest Kings" intersect is their discussion of genealogy. To quote the contents of the scrapbook article on this subject:

> "The writings in the tomb," commented Dr. Lao Chin, the Chinese archaeologist associated with the Kozloff expedition, "are the books of a golden age. In the secret chambers of the old Tao temples are to be found fragments of the same kind of writing, but no one has been able to decipher them. Once a great white race inhabited

what is now the Gobi. China, India and the Mediterranean countries were then inhabited only by barbarians. These men of the Gobi sent out expeditions to colonize the wilds of a savage earth. Some of them came to China and, mixing with the best of the yellow savages, became the Chinese race[…]"

James description of Chinese civilization beginning on page 224 of the 1931 *Children of Mu* begins with the basic premise above. He continues with a tale pulled from his 19th century mindset to further extend the importance of his Uighur people.

CHINA — The Chinese civilization is referred to and looked upon as one of the very old ones. As a Chinese civilization it dates back only about 5000 years. It is popularly believed that the Chinese themselves developed their civilization. They did not. The Chinese civilization was inherited from their father's side. Again, the Chinaman is looked upon as a Mongol; he is only half Mongol, his forefathers were white Aryans. During the time of the Uighur Empire, many of the white Uighurs intermarried with yellow Mongols whose country lay to the south of the Uighur Empire, and the descendants of these intermarriages formed the first Chinese Empire. The record reads: "Uighur men married the best of the yellow savages." This without question is a mistranslation, for at the time these marriages were taking place, savagery had never been known on the face of the earth, so that what was meant was unquestionably "the yellow inferior race." This is borne out by traditions which say that "the yellow Mongols were much inferior to the Uighurs, their civilization was below that of the Uighurs." Many of the Chinese today, especially the high class, have quite white skins. This is the Uighur blood showing in their veins. The regular Chinese coolie, the lower classes of the Chinese today, have no Uighur blood in them. They are the descendants of the ancient yellow Mongols. The Uighur parents of these intermarriages were very careful to have their children educated up to the Uighur standard, so that when the Chinese Empire was first formed it was by those having Uighur blood in their veins and educated in the Uighur great civilization. The Chinese civilization,

> therefore, was the Uighur civilization handed to them by their fathers. There are many writings in the Chinese Tao temples confirming the foregoing and any Chinese scholar can without question confirm it. Another tradition prominent in China is: "The Chinese did not always live in Asia. They came to Asia from a far-off country towards the rising sun."

James Churchward is not alive to defend his words, nor do we know if he were alive today and knowledgeable, would he have the same beliefs. I, as a human being, easily recognize the obnoxious nature of his pronouncements and find his words to be contrary to everything else I have learned and understood. This passage provides fuel for the racist argument of an ancient white people spreading civilization among all the 'other uncivilized peoples.' In another example of this same argument, James describes the conquest of the advanced white civilization of Mexico and Central America by the Mongols. He denies the real Maya their dignity and birthright with this tale. Declaring their ancient monuments and culture the product of earlier white people erases their hard-won achievements. Likewise, he denies the Chinese Han their birthright in stating their now-gone white forefathers created their civilization. While such misconceptions may have been acceptable in the past ninety or so years, today we should know better. The use of these theories to supplement racist propaganda is one of the nefarious agendas needing to be exposed. The scrapbook article spells out the entire scheme by also including the ancient Uighur colonization of Egypt, India, northern Europe and the Americas in the same paragraph. James spreads the same idea throughout his works and in doing so, contradicts his own theory. The underlying theme of James' tale of the now sunken continent of Mu depends on all people being from that egalitarian civilization. His assertions of only the 'Maya' or the 'Uighur' peoples leaving Mu to colonize the planet and then confronting other peoples, (usually the Mongols,) belie his story of Mu as the 'Garden of Eden.' Even if all those other people were from Mu, why was there a need to dominate or run them off?

Most advocates of James Churchward's theories probably do not recognize the racist undertones contained in his theories; at least that is my hope. To some, his writings inspire a spiritually minded civilization, once as our past and now, as our potential future. In pursuit of that future, the advocates become searchers to regain the now-hidden knowledge. They seek to put humankind on that path to 'Mu' and a special existence where all mankind lives in harmony and peace. It is a lofty goal and racism will not help achieve it. While James' words may inspire searchers, answers leading to the discovery of an ancient advanced civilization do not appear in James' writings. Basic scientific knowledge, however decried and maligned by James, has made significant progress in the last 90 or so years to update our understanding of the physical world and human history. James did not have the luxury of the accurate dating of objects and structures, nor the evidence of the archaeological record uncovered over the past century. To begin a pursuit to find 'the' ancient advanced civilization, it has to start with real data and logical assumptions. Sure, some crazy-sounding theories belong in the mix, albeit with deserved scrutiny and the understanding fantastic theories require fantastic proofs.

The Great Uighur Empire envisioned by my great-grandfather is a fable; an additional item, grabbed from yellow journalism and weaved into the tale of his lost continent of Mu. The Uighur Empire/Khaganate was great in its own right and their descendants, the Taklamakanians (or Uyghur,) do not require a spectacular history to make them special.

Chapter 3: Other Mentions of the Great Uighur Empire

Edgar Cayce (1877 – 1945,) the Sleeping Prophet, mentions the higher civilization of the Gobi along with Atlantis and Lemuria. A Christian Mystic, Cayce was renowned for his readings while in a trance state. Shirley Andrews in *Lemuria and Atlantis Studying the Past to Survive the Future* uses Cayce's readings to introduce the Uighur Empire to her readers, interspersed with quotes from James Churchward's works. Note the author in the text uses the terms Lemuria and Mu interchangeably. According to Andrews:

> "Edgar Cayce tells us that at an international conference held in 50,722 B.C., representatives from five countries assembled in Atlantis to discuss a permanent solution to the problem of the omnipresent dangerous wild animals that were overrunning the Earth. The Atlanteans provide transportation to their country in what may have been the first flying vehicles, airships that contained gas and resembled balloons. [1 Cayce, Readings 953-24] People from Lemuria, the Uighur Empire in the Gobi, west and north Africa, and the Carpathian Mountains of central Europe came to the first conference. Delegates from Peru and India were included in later meetings[...] Atlantean priestesses frequently traveled to the distant land of the Uighurs to minister to the people and teach them the power of right and wrong. [15 Cayce, Readings 1273-1, 1648-1, 3420-1] They worked together with the Lemurians, who joined them to teach the tenets of the Law of One[...] Cayce's references to a City of Gold, a Temple of Gold, and a Temple of the Sun in Mongoloid land [17 Cayce, Readings 1648-1] lend support to the Chinese legends that describe the prosperity of the Uighur Empire in the Gobi in the distant past."

As mentioned, her supporting material provided from James' works includes references to Russian explorers uncovering the ruins of Khara Khota and the already listed advanced accomplishments the ancient civilization revealed to Kozlov. Andrews also references the image of the 'Uighur Queen and her

Consort,' however the meaning of the trident held by the Queen no longer represents the symbol of Mu. Her description relates the 'ancient painting' as memorializing the two cultures (Lemuria and Atlantis.) The Queen holds Poseidon's trident, the symbol of Atlantis; the lotus buds upon which they sit represents Mu. Unfortunately, even though 'quoted' from James' work, his interpretation is changed to match her agenda.

Cayce's international conference to address the problem of dangerous wild animals most likely describes the effort to eradicate the threat of marauding dinosaurs. While most scientific evidence indicates the end of the dinosaurs some tens of millions of years ago, some individuals and organizations still embrace the idea of the coexistence of humans and dinosaurs. James includes petroglyphs he identifies as showing dinosaurs in his books; he believed men and dinosaurs were concurrent on this earth. Some ninety years ago, belief in the concept was more widespread and almost accepted as a testament of faith. In addressing the idea of the flying machines used to transport the delegates, namely, the 'airships that contained gas and resembled balloons,' the concept differs from the flying machines or 'vimana' James describes. His flying ships, vimanas, or 'celestial cars' were self-propelled using the advanced technology of Mu. They had unlimited power and capable of maintaining flight until the hardware wore out.

Another advocate of the ancient Great 'Uigur' Empire was Baird Thomas Spaulding (1872-1953.) In the 1927, *Life and Teaching of the Masters of the Far East* Volume 2, Spaulding declared:

> It is claimed that the Great Uigur Empire existed where the Himalayas and the Gobi are today; that large cities of a people in a high state of civilization existed there and that drifting sand covered the ruins after they were destroyed by the water.

Beginning in 1924, Spaulding related his interactions in the Far East with the ancient Masters in his four volumes entitled *Life and Teaching of the Masters of the Far East.* (Volumes 5 and 6 were published posthumously from earlier articles.) In his works, he acquaints the reader with the ancient, immortal beings he met with his ten companions on their journey through Tibet and India. During their stay with the 'Masters,' the party observed their ability to perform special powers as a normal course of their daily lives. Spaulding relates feats such as walking on water and other acts similar to those attributed to Jesus of Nazareth in the Christian bible. Knowing your 'true' self was the secret to obtaining these powers and the highest form of enlightenment came from realization of the Christ consciousness within yourself.

During the period of his alleged interactions with the Masters (1894,) Spaulding held jobs as a mechanically inclined mining engineer in Alaska, and subsequently California and Montana. While inconvenient to his narrative, it probably precludes his participation in the purported Asian expedition. One might ask why Spaulding waited thirty years to bring the astonishing information learned from the 'Masters' to the public. The same applies to James who waited more than forty-five years to publicize his knowledge of the Naacal Brotherhood and the lost continent of Mu.

One thing is known for sure; Baird and Stella Spaulding were friends with James Churchward and acquainted with his works. The first volume of the *Life and Teaching of the Masters of the Far East* (1924) has no mention of the lost continent of Mu. However, some of James' theories appear in the second (1927) and third (1935) volumes, such as the Naacal Brotherhood and that Moses' words in the Christian bible were mangled translations of the sacred teachings brought from the Motherland, without mentioning Mu by name. Other similarities are the once-fertile plains of the Gobi desert ruled by the advanced Uigur civilization and the relatively late date for the raising of the Earth's mountains.

My research has also revealed Stella Spaulding typed the unpublished book, *Mu's Colonies and Colonial Empires*, from James' handwritten copy. I have James' cover, partial table of contents and some pages from this volume graciously provided by Stella's relatives. I have been unable to obtain a copy of the entire work, but believe it is an unabridged version of the 1931 *Children of Mu.* From the same source, I also have a February 1926 letter from James to Stella Spaulding requesting her husband show his prepared manuscripts to his publisher and provide advice on having them published. He names his other manuscripts as *The Origins and Workings of the Great Forces*, *Geological Phenomena*, and

Volcanic Gases and Their Workings. Obviously, the titles changed over time, but later that year (1926,) W.E Rudge published *Lost Continent of Mu Motherland of Men* and not Spaulding's publisher, DeVorss & Company. A signed copy of the 1926 book given to the Spauldings bears the inscription "Cordially yours" with another inscription to Stella reading, "With the compliments and kind wishes of J Churchward."

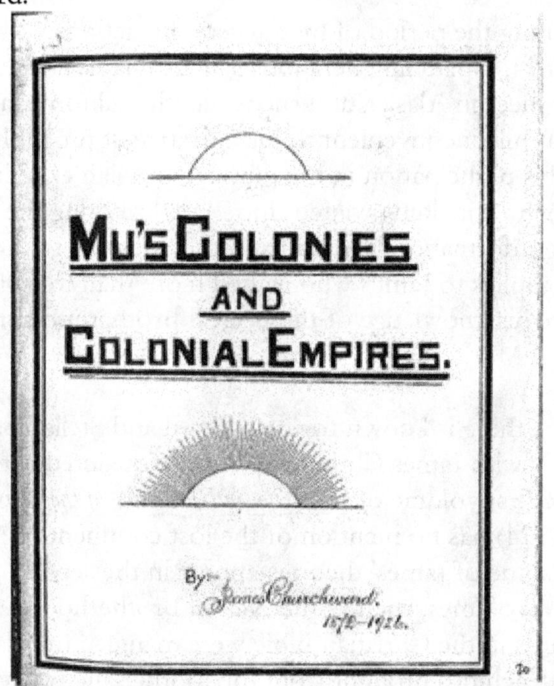

Figure 20: Cover of *Mu's Colonies and Colonial Empires*

Contained in James' scrapbooks are two letters from Stella Spaulding, both written in the summer of 1926. According to the June 30th letter:

> "At last the book has arrived and we vote it a beauty. Mr. Spaulding's appreciation is shown by the way he spends every spare moment within its covers. He finds so much he has been interested in for so long."

It is possible Spaulding learned the same truths during his time in the Far East as James had, however one can point to Spaulding's interest in and access to James' theories prior to the first inclusion of coincidental material.

With the prominence James placed on the Great Uighur Empire, perhaps an extended version of his chapter in *Mu's Colonies and Colonial Empires* would provide further information on the Great Uighur Empire and his source material.

Figure 21: Dr. Jozsef Cserep

Another reference to the Uighur is contained in the translation of letters to James Churchward from Dr. Jozsef Cserep self-identified as a Professor of the University of Budapest, Hungary. Dr. Cserep exchanged correspondence with James in the late 1920s. The information I have on Cserep is very thin; from email correspondence I learned he was a professor of Latin, Greek and Hungarian and conducted research in Italy and Greece for the Hungarian government. My letters to the University of Budapest requesting further information have gone unanswered.

One of the two passages mentioning the Uighur in Cserep's Magyar language letter entitled, "*America as the Prehistoric Cradle of the Caucasian Race*" appears to support the possibility of the Uighur as the forebears of the Hungarian people, which conflicts with medieval Hungarian sources. The proponents of the former theory believe the westward Uighur migration brought them to settle in today's Hungary. Cserep relates the following:

> "The classical traditions of antiquity, however, did not allow us any clear conception about the Skytha origin of the Huns, who were nomads and in other respects were rather similar to the ALANS, but with regard to morality and methods of life were inferior to them. (See Ammianus Marcellinus XXI,20,21)
>
> The only one Hun word we know until today, "strava," (= banqueting feast) has a rather "Slavonic" flavor. Notwithstanding the possibility cannot be excluded, that they were a branch of those OUIGHUR (Uighur) race to which also belong the race of the Turks, since the OUIGHURS, according to Col. J. Churchward, were western colonists of the submerged continent of MU, who migrated to Asia still before the disappearance of that great continent, and also later they continued their western migrations.
>
> *America as the Prehistoric Cradle of the Caucasian Race*, page 28

Unfortunately, two pages later, Cserep dashes the hopes of the Uighur-Magyar connection with the following:

> After the destruction of their empire in the VI. Century B.C. the Mede people migrated to the plains between the rivers Don and Volga, certainly with the aim of saving themselves from the total destruction by the victorious Skytha-Persians.- There they lived under the names of MAGYAR and SARMATA during several centuries, until the pression from beyond the Volga river, suffered from the OUIGHUR-HUN-TURK tribes, compelled them to migrate toward West and Southwest and ultimately about the year of 886 immigrated to the present days' Hungary, where they met the other branch of the prehistoric Madya people, the PAIONS or Pannons who lived there already for 1600 years together with the brother tribes of MESSIANI, like the chronicles called the Myz-Meron people, the SZEKELY people of Transsylvania and the EMATHIAN (=Matyo) people which lived on the Balkan already in the neighborhood of the Paions.
>
> *America as the Prehistoric Cradle of the Caucasian Race*, page 30

According to a Hungarian legend dating back to the late 13th century, the ancestors of the Hungarian people were Hunor and Magor and born in Scythia. Their descendants included Attila and Prince Almos, father of Prince Arpad. The legend also claims Arpad led the Hungarian conquest of the Carpathian Basin in the 10th century; essentially reclaiming the former lands of the Huns and their birthright as Huns. The Huns, an early nomadic people, roamed the Eurasian Steppe and became a thorn in the side of the Roman Empire in the 4th and 5th centuries CE. Historians trace their entry into Europe from among the Scythian peoples known as the Alans. Other scholars place the Huns as related to the migrating Xiongnu-nu from Mongolia, tracing archaeological evidence along a plausible route from Mongolia, through Central Asia and on to Eastern Europe.

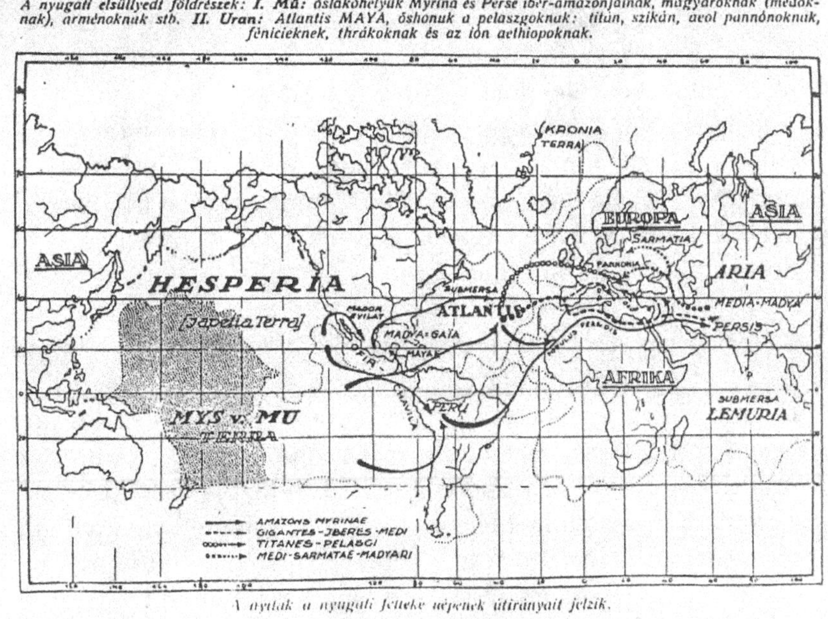

Figure 22: Jozsef Cserep's 1933 map

Curiously, there is a proposed link from ancient Sumer to the Magyar. Some research into the early 18th century archaeological discoveries from Sumer has indicated similarities between the Sumerian language and the Ural-Altaic language group (Hungarian, Turkic, Mongolian, and Finnic.) The five thousand-year-old texts found during the excavations are the earliest known writing and when compared to the earliest form of Hungarian grammar are purportedly quite similar. Kalman Gosztony, author of *Sumerian Etymological Dictionary and Comparative Grammar* found 51 out of 53 characteristics of Sumerian grammar match those of the Hungarian language. Compared to 29 matches for Turkic languages; his research indicates Hungarian appears to have a closer link with the earliest known form of written language. Of course, other linguistic studies comparing their ancient language are likewise an attempt to seize the nationalistic throne of the most ancient civilization. In truth, no verifiable link has been found.

Jozsef Cserep's historical commentary describes a time many thousands of years after the 'Tertiary' migration of the Uighur posited by Churchward and by referencing James' theory, he seriously damages his credibility. Perhaps Cserep read a mistranslation of James writings. Cserep's description of nomadic peoples from Asia crossing the Volga River and into Western Europe somewhat follows the Hungarian legend of Hunor and Magor and even has some confirmation from archaeological evidence. Over a thousand years ago, the differences in dress and cultures of the nomadic people of Inner Asia would be hardly noticeable. Their ancestors could be from the Uighur and just as likely to be Hun, Basmil, Karluk, or Gok-Turk; all of whom dressed alike and had similar customs.

While discussing the Magyar, mention should be made of the *Arvisura*, a written 'ancient' history of the Magyar. A partial English-language translation provided by a reader relates the tome begins with a Pacific Ocean continent named Ataisz. The now sunken continent's description is similar to Plato's description of Atlantis and asserts the Magyars began civilization there. According to the map provided, the early Magyar migrated both toward the east to Central America and west to southern Asia and Mesopotamia after a great cataclysm in 7000 BC. They arrived in Mesopotamia in 4040 BC, formed an association of 24 tribes, and began to document the history of the Magyar, the basis of the Arvisura.

Background on the Arvisura indicates Paal Zoltan wrote the detailed history in the mid-twentieth century. During a 'feast of the bear' ritual and after the consumption of a magical beverage, his shamanistic powers awakened. His awakening permitted him to create the *Arvisura* and relate the history of the Magyar people. The story contains many of the elements found in James Churchward's stories, without the same names, and written to uplift the spirits of a Magyar audience.

The mass republication of James' books arrived in paperback in the 1960s and the original canon expanded by two, given the popularity of his theories. One is an admitted hoax, first published in 1970 called *Revealing Mu* by Tony Earll (an anagram of 'not really'.) Written by the late Raymond Buckland (1934 -2017,) better known for his books on Witchcraft and Wicca, the story tells of the then-recent discovery of tablets describing the exploits of Kland, a neophyte in the Naacal Brotherhood living in the land of Mu. The second, also published in 1970, provided an updated refinement of James' theories under the title, *Understanding Mu*. The author was Hans Stefan Santesson (1914 – 1975,) an American editor, writer and associated with Science Fiction and Fantasy subjects. One chapter is devoted to the Uighurs and repeats the same material; however, Santesson does so without the air of superiority in the original. His account is almost skeptical and instead of offering supporting facts, the author points out where James' argument is thin. He also mentions the inconvenient fact James never identifies those locations where he discovered his evidence.

Statements declaring the Uighur built the 'ancient pyramids' near Xian, China is another embellishment of Churchward's legend of the Great Uighur Empire. Staring with Churchward's theory, the mythology sprouts a new branch to include standing monuments and the suggestion of an historical cover-up. Using James' written words in response, the north running wave destroyed the eastern half of the Uighur Empire and this would have included most, if not all, of China. Therefore, using James' theories, these 'ancient pyramids' must not date from the time of the Uighur, prior to the great Magnetic Cataclysm. Using historical records, Xian was the capital of the Han Chinese state during the Qin (221 – 206 BCE) followed by the Western Han (206 BCE – 220 CE) and the Tang (618 – 907 CE.) Thirty-eight pyramidal-shaped mausoleums and burial mounds of Chinese Emperors and their relatives lie scattered throughout the countryside near Xian. The most famous is the

Mausoleum of the first Qin Emperor, Qin Shi Huang (259 – 210 BCE) and his standing army of Terracotta Warriors. Described by Chinese historian Sima Qian (145 – 90 BCE) in the *Records of the Grand Historian* only a century later, the building of the mausoleum eventually involved 700,000 workers and held wondrous objects. The nearby 'Great White Pyramid,' claimed to be built by aliens or the Uighur is known to be the Maoling Mausoleum of Emperor Wu of Han (156 – 87 BCE). Just as history recorded these Emperor's interactions with the Xiongnu (see page 12,) it also recorded the circumstances of these pyramidal shaped structures and the archaeological record agrees. Some of the 'pyramids' attract tourists where museums display the artifacts discovered from excavations, most notably the Terra-cotta warriors, standing guard for more than two-thousand years. While a casual glance at James' works might attribute these ancient structures to the Great Uighur Empire reaching its height 17,000 years ago, real Chinese historical records and archaeological evidence indicates their true circumstances; the resting places for Chinese Emperors and their relatives.

In 2010, an ethnic Uyghur from Kazakhstan visited my home to speak with me concerning the central Asian healing system known as Elle Ayat. Due to the Kazakhstan court's decision to outlaw the practice, I withhold his name. Speaking through a Russian translator, the visitor stated he came to speak with me personally because of my research into my great-grandfather's theories and the assumed continuation of their promulgation. I learned Abdulla Farhata Mohammed Obicha(sp) or simply Farhata-ata, born in Ghulja (Yining) in the Xinjiang Uygur Autonomous Region, People's Republic of China, discovered the healing system. His Uyghur heritage and genetics permitted him to access information harkening back to the Great Uighur Empire as described by James Churchward. He provided a mantra for his followers to chant while staring into the sun. The mantra permitted the consciousness of the world to change through the mind-to-mind connections of the people of Earth. The goal is the recreation of the Great Uighur Empire as envisioned by my great grandfather. Additional benefits of the practice bring good health and riches, not just to the practitioner, but also to their friends and relatives. The visitor was very emphatic; Elle Ayat has no affiliation with any religious or political organization. I also learned Farhata-ata also once held a copy of one of the James' books and declared it was 80% accurate. One of the questions he asked of me was a clarification on the Russian translation of James' books regarding the Great Uighur Empire. Apparently, there is a difference between the English language version and the Russian translation on a few points. I am not surprised the 'pravda' version is different considering the ongoing propaganda war when it was probably translated. The visitor also requested to conduct a ceremony where I would stare into the sun while he chanted the mantra; my participation lasted as long as I could stand looking into the sun. A subsequent visit in 2015 by an English-speaking proponent followed, thankfully during the evening. Medical advice indicates staring into the sun is detrimental to one's health and I have not repeated it, nor would I suggest the practice for anyone else.

James Churchward's account of the Great Uighur Empire also helped fuel political change. In the early days after the formation of the Republic of Turkey, Mustafa Kemal Ataturk (1881-1938) sent historian Tahsin Mayatepek to Mexico City to act as the Turkish charge' d' affairs. The documentation of Mayatepek's efforts is detailed in Turkish records and literature with scant translations into English I have found available. Mayatepek researched the similarities between Maya and Turkish words and culture, finding apparent links between the two peoples. In 1936, Mayatepek sent copies of some of James' books back to Ataturk for consideration and the copies subsequently translated into Turkish. According to my 'informants,' a museum houses the original volumes with highlights and comments in the margins under protected glass. According to M Sukru Hanioglu, author of *Ataturk: An Intellectual Biography*, Ataturk believed James' writings confirmed the Sun Language theory and an ancient Turkish past. Churchward's linking of supposedly Turkic runes with the symbols he discovered on the Naacal tablets in India and their identification as Uighur gave credence to the idea Turks brought civilization to the world, including the Americas. The idea also established a non-religious history to the new secular government of the Republic of Turkey, rising from the ashes of the Ottoman Empire. Their leap into the twentieth century to join the growing number of nations basing their governance on equality under the rule of law and representative democratic principles provided a new identity, free from religious influence. Unfortunately, things change over time.

The Sun Language theory proposed all human languages have a common ancestry in a proto-Turkic primal language developed in Central Asia. Evidently, a group of sun-worshippers decided to form language to honor the Sun, hence the name Sun Language. The hypothesis is widely regarded in the West as Turkish nationalist pseudoscientific nonsense. In corresponding with Turkish friends about the role James Churchward played in Ataturk's ideas, many complain about the Western conspiracy to silence proponents of Turkish history and are afraid to comment. On the other hand, some Turkish authors embrace the concept and keep it alive. Sinan Meydan wrote *Atatürk ve Kayıp Kıta Mu* (*Ataturk and the Lost Continent Mu.*) My correspondence with Sinan Meydan was fruitless and I have yet to find an English translation of his book; I am sure it would be informative. I obtained a list of the names of other advocates, but other than one, I have yet to find English language material to create a proper discussion of their ideas. This brings up Polat Kaya.

> Polat Kaya believes:
> "The ancient Turanian civilization was a world wide civilization. It has been referred to as the "Turkish Era" (Tarih-i Türk) in history,"
> and
> "It seems that until some 3000 years ago from present, the world spoke one language and that one language was Turkish. I have analyzed many non-Turkish words with their given meanings and found that embedded in them were Turkish words or expressions with the same meaning - or a similar meaning - which cannot be due to coincidence.
> The ancient world was dominated by the Turkish speaking Turanians, and Turkish was the dominant language that the world was speaking[…]"
> http://polatkaya.net/Sun_Empire_of_Ancient_India.html; downloaded 2017-11-26

Mr. Kaya has an online repository of his writings at polatkaya.net. I was once a member of a Yahoo Group where he would provide new articles concerning the English words he discovered stolen from the Turkish language. His website also has an archive of the Yahoo postings. To uncover these stolen words, his method involves rearranging letters and finding Turkish words close to the rearranged letters. Sometimes, he replaces and adds letters to make it consistent with the phonetic spelling. I found it difficult to understand his analysis within the confines of scientific reasoning. First, he submits everyone spoke a common tongue, Turkish. If everybody spoke Turkish only 3,000 years ago, why are there so many different language families today? Why are all the stolen words in English? Since he also states Turkish was the dominant language, what language were the 'barbarians' speaking?

Polat Kaya's efforts to identify the stolen words becomes his proof of the conspiracy to suppress 'real' Turkish history; by 'hiding' Turkish words in other languages, the 'barbarians' have acknowledged the Turk's unique historical status as the civilizing influence on all of humanity. Because western scholars reject the Sun Language theory and the hidden words, they are complicit in the conspiracy to hide the true creators of civilization.

Kaya's posting on the word 'knucklehead' became the final straw for me. Reproduced below is his analysis:

> Here is an interesting word in English that needs to be explored for its make up. It is the English word "knucklehead" that means "a stupid person", [Oxford American Dictionaries].
>
> When this English word KNUCKLEHEAD is rearranged letter-by-letter as "CUH-DANKELEK" or "CUK-DANKELEH" and the deciphered word is read as in Turkish, it becomes obvious that it is an anagrammatized and Anglicized form of the Turkish expression "ÇOK DANGALAK" meaning "very stupid, blockhead, knucklehead". Clearly, this Turkish expression "ÇOK DANGALAK" has been stolen and used to manufacture this English word KNUCKLEHEAD. Thus, this is another example that, regarding the authenticity of "Indo-European" languages, the Turks and the rest of the world public have been misled by the manufacturers and presenters of such languages.
>
> Of course, by such activities, not only are the Turkish language words and expressions stolen, but also the linguistic creations of the Turkish people, hence, Turkish civilization is stolen. This kind of stealing from the ancient

Turanian language of Turkish and the ancient Turanian civilization has been going on since the time of the Babylonians, that is, for at least the last 4,000 years. The truth about world languages is not as it appears - or as it is presented to us. Linguistically, this cannot be ignored. It is time that linguists who work on the "etymology" of words to take note of this ongoing deception.

In looking up the etymology of 'knucklehead,' I discovered the word started use in World War 2 among American GIs. To me, the idea of a group of GIs sitting around stealing words from the Turkish language while fighting a war seems ludicrous. I am sure their priorities would dictate paying attention to staying alive rather than attempting to steal words. My subsequent communications with Mr. Kaya proved fruitless in the effort to point out his illogical analysis; his first reply started as follows:

> I have written about words that are more than 2000 years old and still shown that they were manufactured from Turkish. The "70 years" you keep talking about has no bearing on the anagrammatization process. So this argument of yours is faulty. I can see that you have a problem in accepting what I am demonstrating - but that is your problem - definitely not mine!

Please note the posting dates to 2010, approximately 70 years after World War 2. His website contains an archive of all his postings, including our email exchanges and the My-Mu.com blog has an entire post concerning this issue.

Turkish author Dr. Haluk Berkman, a writer not on the original list of people to contact, in an online paper writes:

> The ancient population of Eurasia speaking the proto-language was the people known as the Uygur (Uighur) whom we know are of Turkic ancestry. The Uighur population formed chains of settlements across central Asia and Central Europe many thousand years ago. Although the historical records claim that the Uighur people are the offspring of the Huns and starts from 300 BCE, the exact beginning date of this culture is much more ancient and very much unclear. One should be very careful in naming ancient cultures. This is because a name is

immediately linked to a certain time period and subjective feelings of possession trigger unending controversies. The approximate starting date of the Ancient Uighur Empire, or more correctly loose federation of independent tribes, could tentatively be located around 20,000 years BP.

It was first James Churchwald (1852-1936), a British officer who served in India during the 1880'ies who brought the Ancient Uighur Empire to the attention of the world. He claimed that a lost continent named Mu existed once upon a time. As the continent located in the middle of the Pacific Ocean disappeared under the sea due to some cataclysmic disaster, people of this culture migrated to distant locations of the world. Their largest and most important colonial empire was the Ancient Uygur Empire, the Empire of the Sun. Churchwald claims: "Next to Mu herself, the Uighur Empire was the largest empire the world has ever known"(1).

Churchwald wrote several books on Mu (2), but as of today (2009) the sunken Mu continent has not been discovered. Nevertheless, the Ancient Uighur federation of tribes is a fact and can be demonstrated to have existed for a rather long period of time. This culture did not totally disappear from the face of the world, but has mutated and evolved into several different nations speaking several interrelated languages. Let us ponder on the main climatic changes which forced these tribes to move out of Central Asia and spread all over the world.

"Ancient Uighur Empire"; Dr. Haluk Berkman; http://www.astroset.com/bireysel_gelisim/ancient/a1.htm ; accessed 2017-11-21

Berkman also includes James' Uighur Empire map from the *Lost Continent of Mu Motherland of Men* page 105. Readers will recognize the influence of James Churchward's Great Uighur Empire with a few differences later in his text. Rather than maintain Churchward's theory of the Indo-European/Aryan genealogy of the Uighur, Berkman identifies them as of Turkic stock and speaking the Turkic proto-language. Additionally, he states, "the Turks were also known under the name of Mu." Berkman elucidates the connection between James Churchward's Great Uighur Empire and the Sun Language theory, although slightly different from Churchward's version. The substitution of a Turkic identity for James' Indo-European/Aryan identity probably resides in the mistranslation of James' works or linking today's Uyghur as the same Uighur from James' Empire.

Even though these proponents use Churchward's writings as evidence of their theories, mentioned by name or not, they contradict him. I should also mention James' theory stated all people were from Mu, not just the Turks, who are actually never mentioned in his books.

My study of the Great Uighur Empire as envisioned and documented by my great-grandfather indicates his written works have had a profound influence. While there are major gaps in my research about all the references to support these theories, I believe it is a fanciful tale. Unfortunately, this fanciful tale offers proof for racist and/or nationalistic theories in the minds of some people and thereby justifies their beliefs in the superiority of 'us' vs. 'them.'

I submit James' works when originally published served as escapist literature. His writings provided hope among people suffering from the effects of the Great Depression. In reading his works, they were heirs of a great advanced civilization and with his 'new' knowledge could escape the peril of their age. How much is different today with open religious and sectarian warfare and the newly re-added threat of nuclear annihilation? If we are to search for an ancient advanced civilization to escape the pressures of our existence and solve all the world's problems it must be with the understanding no advancement in technology will 'do the trick.' Advanced agriculture will feed the soldiers of swelling armies for further conquest; advanced weaponry will kill people faster, but not feed the starving. Technology is not the answer to our ills.

If there is anything in James' works to salvage, it is that we are all related. Sometimes forgotten is the common bond we share as humans on our planet. We can reshape our world as soon as we all remember our place as citizens of the Earth and act in the best interests of our people and planet.

Appendices

Appendix 1: 'Uighur' in the 1926 *Lost Continent of Mu Motherland of Men*

Chapter V - THE EGYPTIAN SACRED VOLUME, BOOK OF THE DEAD
pages 105-110

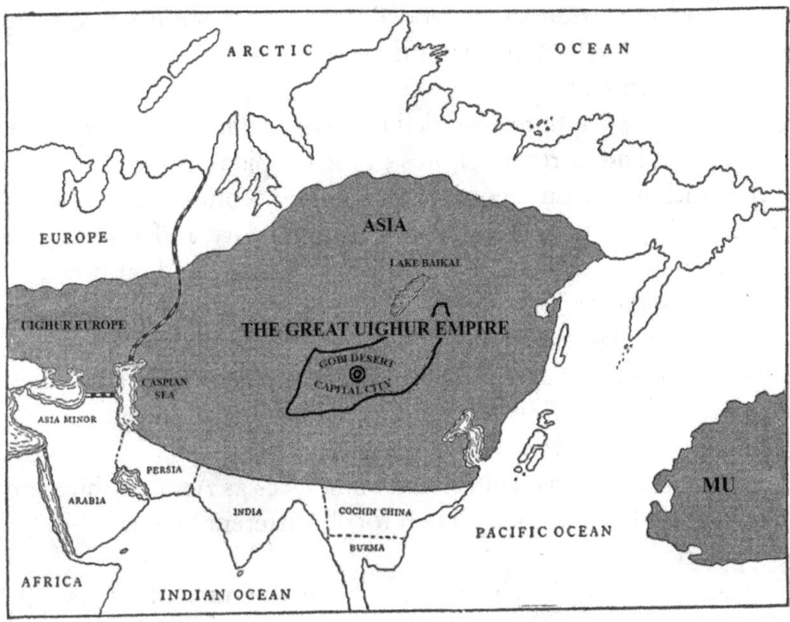

Map of the Great Uighur Empire

I think the Uighur records will be all that is necessary to convince the most skeptical mind that it is clearly proven by symbols alone that Mu was the motherland of man; but, as an old Hindu saying goes:

"It is easier to snatch a pearl from the teeth of a crocodile, or to twist an angry, venomous serpent around one's head like a garland of flowers, without incurring danger, than to make an Ignorant or an obstinate person change his mind."

The Uighur was the principal colonial empire belonging to Mu at the time of the biblical "Flood," which destroyed its eastern half.

Chinese legends tell that the Uighurs were at the height of their civilization about 17,000 years ago. This date agrees with geological phenomena.

The Uighur Empire stretched its powerful arms from the Pacific Ocean across Central Asia and into Eastern Europe from the Caspian Sea on. This was before the British Isles became separated from the continent of Europe.

The southern boundary of the Uighur Empire was along the northern boundaries of Cochin China, Burma, India and Persia, and this was before the Himalayas and the. other Asiaitic mountains were raised.

Their northern boundary extended into Siberia, but how far there is no record to tell. Remains of their cities have been found in the southern parts of Siberia.

Eventually the Uighurs extended themselves into Europe around the western and northern shores of the Caspian Sea, as related in a very ancient Hindu record; from here they continued on through Central Europe to its western boundary, Ireland.

They settled in northern Spain, northern France, and far down into the Balkan region. The late archaeological discoveries in Moravia are Uighur remains, and the evidences on which ethnologists have based their theories that man originated in Asia, have been marks left by the advancing Uighurs in Europe.

The history of the Uighurs is the history of the Aryans.

Ethnologists have classed certain white races as Aryans which are not Aryans at all, but belong to a totally different line of colonization.

The capital city of the Uighurs was where the ruins of Khara Khoto now stand in the Gobi Desert. At the time of the Uighur Empire the Gobi Desert was an exceedingly fertile area of land.

The Uighurs had reached a high state of civilization and culture: they knew astrology, mining, the textile industries, architecture, mathematics, agriculture, writing, reading, medicine, etc. They were experts in decorative art on silk, metals and wood, and they made statues of gold, silver, bronze and clay; and this was before the history of Egypt commenced.

About one-half of the Uighur Empire was destroyed before Mu went down, the other half subsequent to Mu's submersion.

Professor Kozloff unearthed a tomb 50 feet below the surface at Khara Khoto and in it found wonderful treasures, which he photographed, not being allowed to disturb or take anything away. Through the courtesy and kindness of the *Sunday American* I have obtained the loan of some of these pictures, two of which I here reproduce with their decipherings, as they are symbolical. I

Loaned from the Collection of the American Weekly Section of the New York Sunday American.
AN UIGHUR QUEEN AND HER CONSORT

SCEPTER CARRIED BY A MONARCH OF THE UIGHURS
Of later date than that shown in the hand of the Queen. Both show the trident

think I am safe in believing that these pictures represent a time between 16,000 and 18,000 years ago.

These pictures are symbolical, the various symbols telling who they are, and what they are. In the original they are paintings on silk and represent a queen and her consort in a sitting posture. I will now pick out the symbols of the Queen. On her head is a three-pointed crown with a disc in the center with three sets of rays emanating from it. Behind her body is a large disc, the sun. At the back of her head is a smaller disc, an inferior sun. The large disc symbolizes Mu, the small disc the Uighur Colonial Empire. The crown on her head, a sun with rays on one half only, shows the escutcheon of a colonial empire. In her left hand she carries a scepter, the ends of which are in the form of a trident—three points—the Motherland's numeral.

Her seat is a full-blown sacred lotus, the floral symbol of the Motherland, so that she is depicted as sitting in the lap of and being upheld by Mu, the Motherland. Her consort does not carry a scepter, nor has he a sun with rays, but in its place a sphere. His crown also shows the Motherland's numeral.

Kozloff had pictures of various scepters. This illustration is of a different pattern to the one held in the queen's hand, and of later date, but symbolically reads the same, the ends being divided into three giving the numeral of the Motherland.

Thus we see the symbols of Asia, America, South Sea Islands and New Zealand all agreeing in the tale they tell. Could anything be more definite or convincing—unless we could get our old forefathers to rise from their graves, and tell us by word of mouth what happened to them in the land of Mu?

Chapter 10 - NORTH AMERICANS PLACE AMONG THE ANCIENT CIVILIZATIONS
Page 174

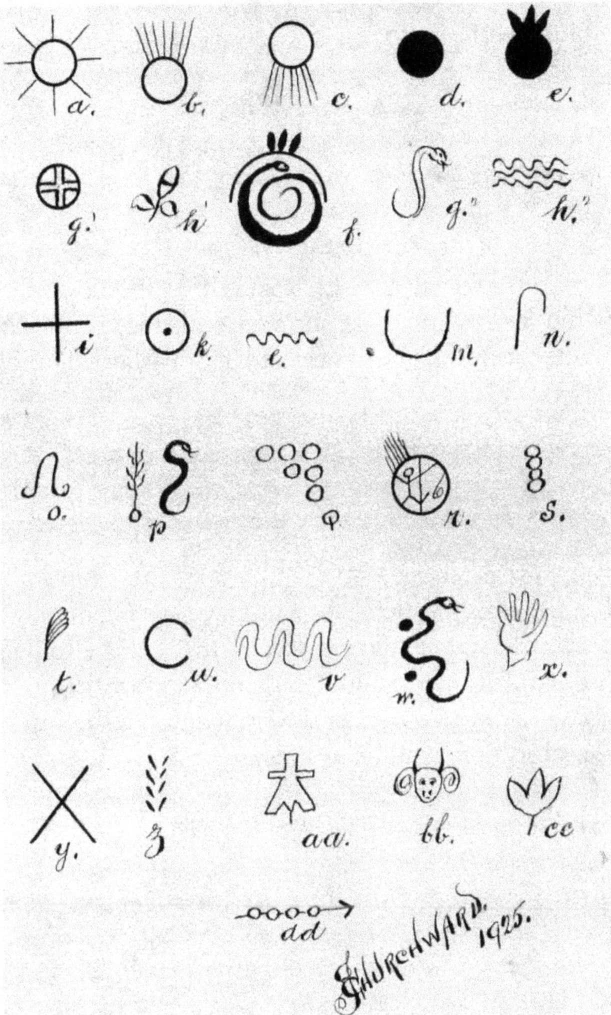

SYMBOLS FOUND AMONG THE CLIFF-DWELLERS' WRITINGS

Page 177
(referencing the previous illustration)

R. This is an Uighur-Maya religious symbol.

S. This is the Uighur hieratic letter *h*.

Page 182

CLIFF DWELLERS' GUIDEPOST

CLIFF DWELLERS' GUIDEPOST

... From the main symbol are shown streams joining each other. The characters on this picture are all Uighur-Maya. These people may have been Mongols....

Chapter 11 - NIVEN'S MEXICAN BURIED CITIES
Page 220 – 225

Through the great courtesy and kindness of the *Dearborn Independent*, Dearborn, Michigan, who have supplied me with cuts of these tablets, I am enabled to give what I believe to be some very valuable information about early man in North America. These tablets are in two forms of writing: pictures composed of symbols, and some Uighur-Maya hier-

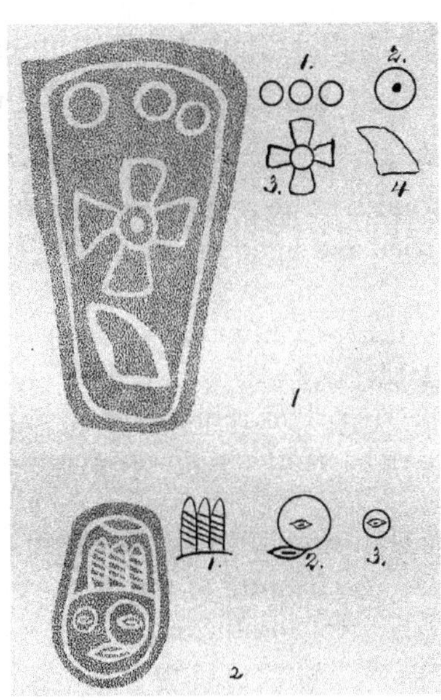

Courtesy of the Dearborn Independent
TABLETS FROM NIVEN'S MEXICAN BURIED CITIES.
SECOND CITY

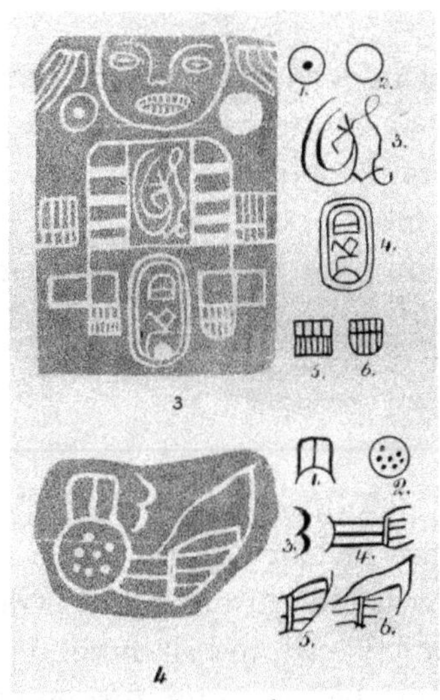

Courtesy of the Dearborn Independent
TABLETS FROM NIVEN'S MEXICAN BURIED CITIES.
SECOND CITY

atic sentences. The Uighur-Maya hieratic alphabet came out of that of the Motherland and includes many of the Motherland's letters without change.

The tablets were found in the remains of the second city and are made of volcanic rock and lined in red.

...

TABLET 3.-FIGs. 1,2,3,4,5 and 6

At the top of this tablet is a face with the two hands outspread in benediction and blessing. This represents the hieratic head of Mu.

Fig. 1. Beneath the right hand is seen the symbol Ahau, King of Kings.

Fig. 2. Beneath the left hand is the symbol of the sun, therefore the King of Kings of the Empire of the Sun. Thus the top of this tablet reads, "Benedictions and blessings on your temple and people from Ra Mu, the king high priest of the Empire of the Sun."

Fig. 3. This is a compound Uighur symbol and appears in the holy of holies of the temple. It reads, "A temple of truth, dedicated to the Sun and under the jurisdiction of the Motherland."

Fig. 4. In this cartouche is shown a colony of Mu. At the top and at the bottom a colony with the word, I think, "Max," but I am not sure about one of the letters.

Fig. 5. This is the symbol of a pillar, reading "In strength."

Fig. 6. This is the symbol of another pillar, reading "To establish." These evidently compare with the Tat Pillars of temples of later date.

Page 268 – 269

Chapter 14 - THE ORIGIN OF SAVAGERY

The most conspicuous instance of this sort was the great Uighur Empire of central Asia. The eastern half was destroyed by the waters of the biblical "Flood" and all thereon perished. Afterwards the western half went up, forming the Himalaya and other central Asiatic mountains. Among these mountains were many plateaus, where the people survived and finally worked their way back into various flat countries. Those of the Uighurs who survived were the forefathers of the Aryan races. Both in India and China there are traditions relating to the raising of these mountains, the great loss of life that ensued and the survival of many who lived in the mountains following the great upheaval.

Appendix 2: 'Uighur' in the 1927 *Copies of Stone Tablets Found by William Niven at Santiago Ahuizoctla Near Mexico City*

Pages 1-5

Niven's Mexican Buried Cities.

Near Mexico City, Mexico

In the "Lost Continent of Mu" I gave a description of the discovery of three buried cities one underneath the other discovered by William Niven about 29 miles north of Mexico City.

In this volume I am giving a few details of other buried cities quite close to Mexico City also discovered by William Niven, at suburbs or outskirts of Mexico City called Santiago Ahuizoctla and Hacienda de Leon. There are others in close proximity about which I have not yet received the details.

The remains at Santiago Ahuizoctla and Hacienda de Leon are found at depths of from 10 to 13 feet – from the surface of the land. Niven has taken out over 2000 relics from Buried Cities around Mexico City, comprising some wonderful stone tablets, figures, carvings, etc.

From the meager geological data which I have about these past civilizations, I am of an opinion that this civilization was contemporary with the upper civilization, 29 miles north of Mexico City and mentioned in the "Lost Continent of Mu" and it would also appear that it was the same cataclysmic wave that wiped out both civilizations. They were only 30 miles apart.

Niven places Santiago Ahuizoctla and Hacienda de Leon civilization as existing about 4000 B.C. Mr. Niven is too modest. From the information shown from the decipherings of one of Niven's finds, which decipherings are hereafter given, it is shown, that unquestionably this civilization existed more than 12000 years ago.

Through the great courtesy of William Niven in supplying me with photos and drawings of many tablets which he has found enables me to give my readers a slight insight into this past unknown American civilization.

From the writings on the tablets I can safely say that the people of this buried city were a totally different race from their neighbors the Yucatan Mayas. Neither were these people Uighurs or Nagas.

These people had a writing peculiarly their own. It was composed to a great extent of the hieratic letters and symbols of the Motherland. The balance was composed of glyphs, very much like the Uighur, but not the pure Uighurs of eastern Asia.

From the many and various details shown in the tablets and writings sent to me by Niven, it is quite evident that their territory in the motherland before they migrated was to the east of the Uighurs and north of the Yucatan Mayas and Karas, and yet adjoining the both. Their language and glyphs corroborate this.

From the carvings of figures which Niven found if they really represent the features of the people, these people were of a type unknown to day. Their mouths are their most prominent feature which are large, open, loose and flabby lipped – a really ugly disagreeable mouth. Their general features have a cast of the Mongoloid, but not sufficiently defined to say that they were Mongols. I cannot classify them.

From their writings a few of which I am giving herewith with their decipherings, must convince one that their cosmology was of a high order. They had a monotheistic worship of the deity and made His Four Great Attributes their principal representative symbol. I must now diverge a little to explain who and what the Four Great Attributes or Sacred Four were.

The conception among all ancient people was: - that in the beginning when the Creation of the universe was begun, it commenced by Four Great Commands from the Deity – These commands had various names given them by the various ancients such as:-

The Sacred Four:- The Builders:- The Four Great Kings:- The Four Great Intellectual Commands, the Dhyhan Cohaus or the Four Great Maharajas etc. But by whatever name they were called, these Four Great Building Commands commenced the creation of the universe by bringing law, order and form out of chaos.

From various writings of these peoples I find that they dedicated their temples to the Sacred Four. One inscription reads:-

> "This temple is dedicated to the Great Creator who by His four great commands brought law, form and order out of chaos."

I think this is a fair general reading of their temple dedications. Apparently, occasionally, they vary somewhat in phraseology, yet this apparent variation may be due to faulty or imperfect translation on my part.

The utmost anyone can do in deciphering and translating ancient inscriptions and writings is to get the general meaning. Anyone who says he can decipher and translate ancient writings and inscriptions so as to bring out all minor details is a fraud and a humbug and has no respect for truth.

The Sacred Four was by far the most prominent symbol among these ancient people of Mexico. I have never found it so prominently used anywhere else. The Seven-headed Serpent was equally prominent among the Nagas, and the Egyptian had Isis, the female aspects of the deity as their first call. The Assyrians made the Sacred Four quite prominent of the Four Genii and the Babylonians frequently referred to them.

A great evolution took place in symbolizing the Sacred Four. The first symbol was a plain cross + which ended in the Dhyhan Cohaus, Swastika and winged circle. There were many forms between the beginning and these three other ends…

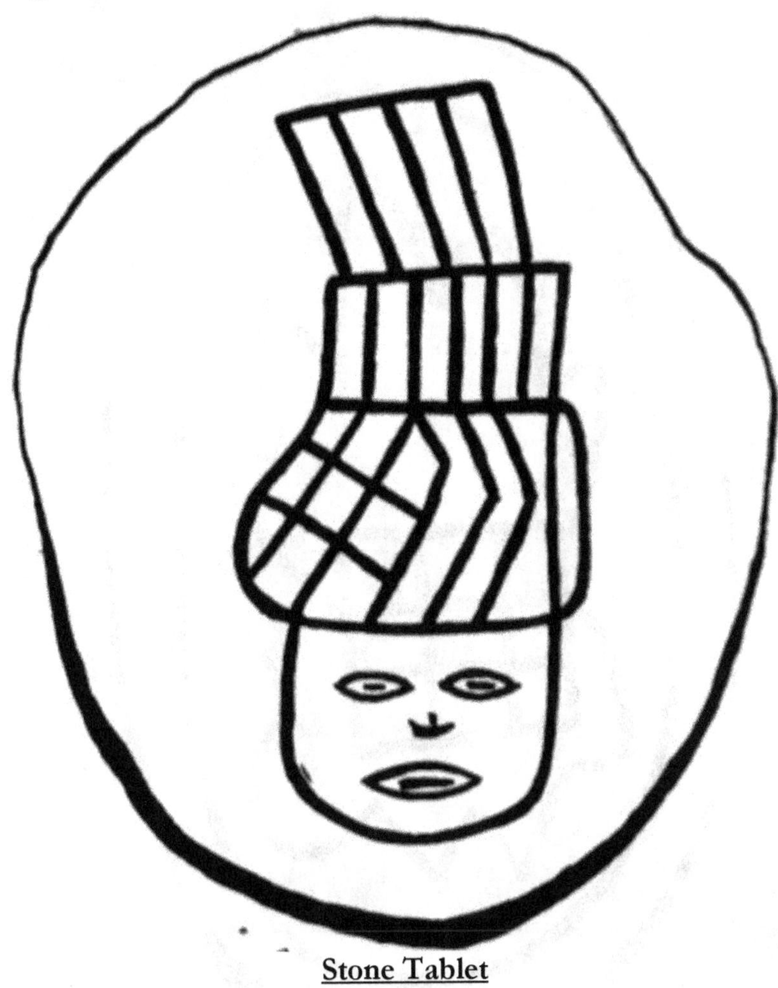

Stone Tablet
From Niven's collection. No. 535

Found at Campala. 6 miles from Mexico City – contains the Uighur symbol for 'God's Field.'

Stone Tablet
From Niven's collection No 921

Found at Chimpala 6 miles from Mexico City
The Uighur symbol for 'God's Field'

Appendix 3: 'Uighur' in the 1927 *Books of the Golden Age*

Book 1: The Sacred & Inspired Writings of Mu
Page 7

The oldest date I can find in connection with the Naacals dates back to 70,000 years ago. There are two tablets bearing this date and both refer to the Naacals carrying their tablets to colonies. One to Ayhodia in India the other to the Capital City of the Uighurs. The Ayhodia tablet is in India and the Uighur Tablet is in Tibet.

Pages 16 – 23 (pagination error – page 19 skipped)

As well as my memory carries me back, the following is the substance and as near as I can remember his words. I do not presume to say that I am uttering my dear old friends exact words for they were spoken more than 40 years ago, unfortunately I did not write them down until many years afterwards. He commenced: -

"The history of Asia contains the history of the earth's greatest calamities that have befallen mankind

More lives have been lost in Asia by great cataclysmic waves, which periodically swept over parts of Asia, than in all of the rest of the world put together: for at one time, Asia throughout was the most thickly populated land on earth. Where the great, bleak, snow-capped mountain ranges now stretch across the land in all directions, were once fertile plains, with man thickly settled upon them.

Hundreds of millions, yes, I think I might say a thousand millions were living on the soil, where the mountain ranges now stretch for thousands of miles, and when the mountains went up, they were nearly all wiped out. Before this great calamity they were living happy contented lives.

During this and earlier in man's history the Holy Brothers the Naacals were active in carrying the wisdom of the Motherland to all parts of the Earth. They left the Motherland with libraries to be left in the various Colonies and Colonial Empires. These libraries were on clay tablets and written in the Motherland by the

College of the Naacals there. They were written in Naga the scientific language of the Motherland and in her hieratic characters and hieratic alphabet, which I have taught you. The tablets carried by the Naacals were principally on religion and cosmic forces. These the Holy Brothers taught the priesthood in the various countries.

There are records of two of these libraries having been carried one to Uighur and one to India over 70,000 years ago. In each country 6 copies were made and given to the temples of six different cities – this made seven cities in each country who had copies of the Sacred Inspired writings.

The set that the legend I am about to relate to you was the set carried to the Capital City of the Uighurs. The vicissitudes which this library has passed through are many and varied. First: - a great flood swept up over the North Eastern parts of Asia wiping out all forms of life and destroying the country over which it swept. The Eastern half of the great Uighur Empire with the capital city were destroyed. The ruins of the temple with the library lay buried beneath many feet of rocks and sand.

Many years afterwards, the legend does not say how long, the Holy Brothers from the western parts of the Empire which had not been touched by the waters came and dug out the library and carried them to a western temple.

NOTE.

(The proofs are very conclusive that this was the biblical 'Flood' and the north running wave of the Last Magnetic Cataclysm. Its range is shown on the accompanying map.)

Then came the time some years afterwards, the legend does not say how long when the mountains were raised. Earthquakes shook the earth to her foundations, it rolled and tore the surface into fragments, rocks were hurled and rolled in all directions. The bowels of the earth were being forced up through her surface. The land rose with rending, crashing detonations, rocks rolled off on all sides as the land went up. All cities, villages and homes were destroyed, and many were buried beneath the debris, very few of the people escaped with their lives, a few out of the hundreds of thousands were saved.

Many many years afterwards, the descendants of some of the Holy Brothers who were saved, came and again rescued the library and carried them to a rock temple at Khanassa where they are to day"

I asked my old friend:- How long ago that the library was brought to its present sanctuary?
He said :- "there is a tradition that they were taken to Khanassa about 8000 to 10,000 years ago"; "there are no written records about it it is all legendary."

Although the destruction of life through the raising of the mountains was appalling, and the greatest sacrifice od human life ever made with the exception of the "Flood," more people escaped with their lives than the legend suggests. There were small communities saved in the mountains where plateaus and broad valleys were formed, because; some thousands of years afterwards the descendants of these communities appeared on the historical stage as strong powerful mountain nations among them the:- Hindu Aryans, Persians, Medes, European Aryans, the Tartars and Mongols.

From the fact the Mongol Tartars and the Manchus came back upon the Eastern parts of the old Uighur Empire, thousands of years after her destruction: intimates that these races formed the Northern people of the Uighur Empire or were an independent people to the north of the Uighur Empire.

During my Asiatic research work I came across a record stating that the Uighur Empire was composed of several little kingdoms, a confederation similar to as many states. I could find no other record corroborating it, so it stands alone. I could find no record that stated that the Uighurs were in any way connected with Mongols except the yellow Mongols at the south of the Empire.

From the fact the Manchus and Tartars appeared where they did, intimates that their forefathers were marooned in the great Altai Range of mountains and not in the Himalayas.

The ancient Uighur Capital City lies under the ruins of the ancient historical city of Khara Khota in the Gobi Desert south of Lake Baikal. In 1906 an explorer named McClelland started to unearth the Capital City. He found between the ruins of Khara Khota and the Capital City a stratum many feet thick composed of boulders, gravel and sand between 40 and 50 feet thick; thus geologically confirming the fact that a destructive cataclysm had passed over and buried the Capital City. It also confirms the legend that the Capital City was destroyed by a "flood."

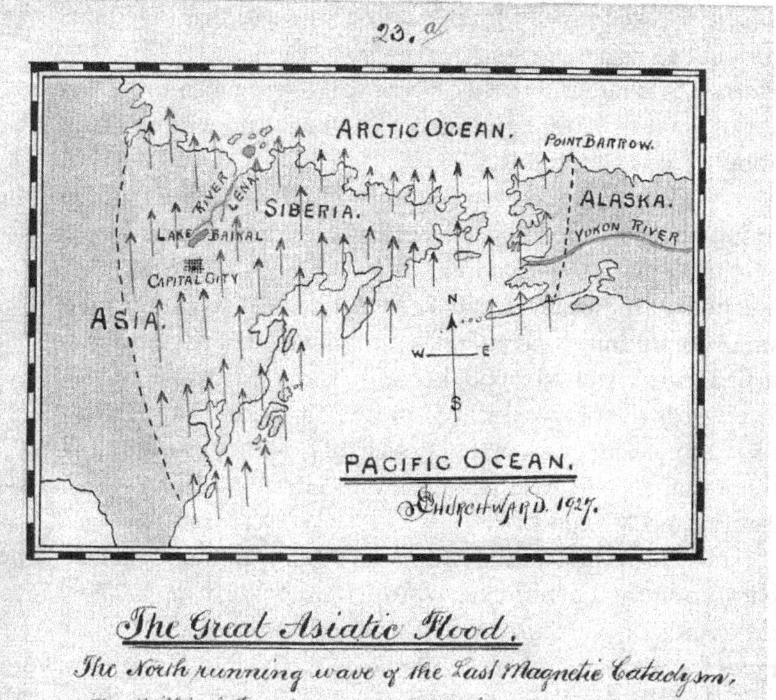

23. a
ARCTIC OCEAN.
POINT BARROW.
ALASKA.
YUKON RIVER
SIBERIA.
LENA RIVER
LAKE BAIKAL
CAPITAL CITY
ASIA.
N
W
E
S
PACIFIC OCEAN.
Churchward. 1927.
The Great Asiatic Flood.
The North running wave of the Last Magnetic Cataclysm, The Biblical Flood and the Geological Myth - The Glacial Period.
Llakoff's Island, the graveyard of the Siberian Mammoth multitudes of them were gathered up, carried there, and there deposited by this flood. The island is composed of their bones.
Site of the Capital City of the Uighurs.
Conventional Map.

The Great Asiatic Flood
The north running wave of the Last Magnetic Cataclysm. The Biblical Flood and the Geological Myth – The Glacial Period.

.Llakoff's Island, the graveyard of the Siberian Mammoth. Multitudes of them were gathered up, carried there and there deposited by this flood. The island is completely composed of their bones.

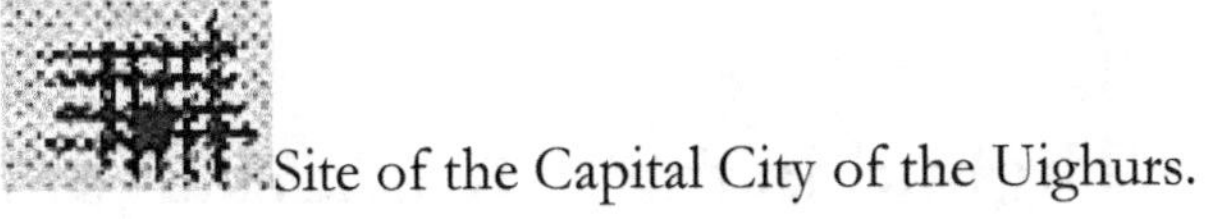
Site of the Capital City of the Uighurs.

Conventional Map

Page 24
<u>Contents of the Tablets</u>

A large portion of the old Uighur library have a date of 70,000 years ago on them. The balance of date from about 70,000 years ago down to about 12,000 to 14,000 years ago. All were written in the Motherland except a small percentage. The tablets containing the Sacred Inspired writings are the oldest of all. They must be over 70,000 years old because they were brought to the Uighur Capital City.

Pages 67 – 68
On one of the latest tablets written, I do not think it came from the Motherland, as the clay is different, gives the locations of the Uighur Capital and six other cities. The general conditions of the country are spoken of – the fertility of the land, the (wads?) canals etc.

Appendix 4: 'Uighur' in the 1931 *Children of Mu*

Chapter II - THE EASTERN LINES
Page 17 – 18
ANCIENT RELICS.—Relics that can be traced back as coming directly from Mu, the Motherland, are extremely rare. During the past few years I have been singularly fortunate in finding two that are at least intimately connected with Mu. Both are symbolic figures in bronze. They were either made in the Motherland or in one of the ancient Uighur cities before the eastern half of that great empire was destroyed by the north running-wave of the last Magnetic Cataclysm which was the Biblical "Flood." This wave destroyed all the country over which it ran, the people were drowned and the cities washed away or buried under the drift. The Uighur Capital City today lies under fifty feet of boulders, gravel and sand. It is situated in the Gobi Desert, which today has large areas of rock only, the soil and everything with it having been washed away by the "Flood."

I am using one of these relics as Plate I (see frontispiece). It is, without question, one of the two oldest bronzes in existence. If Uighur, it is about 18,000 or 20,000 years old. If from Mu, the age cannot be estimated

Courtesy of George N. Leiper

One of the two oldest known bronzes in the world—a symbolical figure of Mu as the mistress and ruler of the whole earth. It was made in either Mu or in the Uighur Capital City over 20,000 years ago.

One of the two oldest known bronzes in the world – a symbolic figure of Mu as the mistress and ruler of the whole earth. It was made in either Mu or in the Uighur Capital City over 20,000 years ago.

This figure is a symbol of Mu as the great ruler. The fineness of the workmanship is not to be found surpassed, and very seldom equaled in any of the prominent jewelry stores in our big cities today. Both symbols have been in America for about 150 years. I know their history, but the less said about it the better, since in the Oriental home from which they were taken, they were without question sacred relics.

Chapter IV - STONE TABLETS FROM THE VALLEY OF MEXICO
Page 55

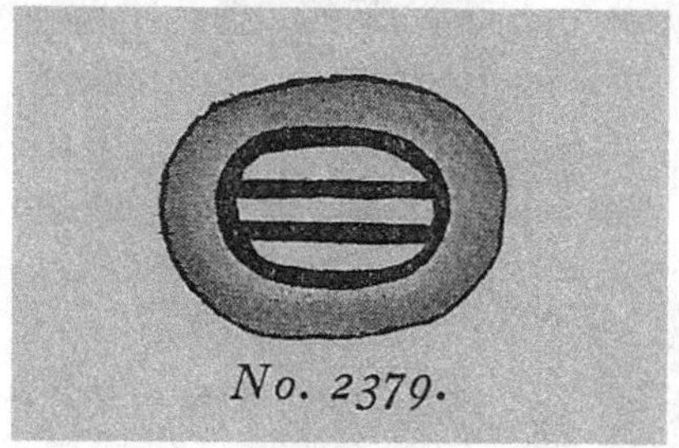
No.2379

THE CREATION OF WOMAN FROM MAN.— A glyph consisting of a circle with two parallel lines drawn through the center, dividing it into three parts, as shown on *Niven's tablet No. 2379*, is a common and universal symbol. It is found among the cliff-dwellers' writings of Nevada. It is found in inscriptions on the Mexican Pyramid at Teotihuacan and in Maya writings. It is to be seen on Inscription Rock, Northeast Brazil, near the boundary of British Guiana, and in various other ancient American carvings. It occurs in the ancient writings of the Uighurs, Hindus, Babylonians and Egyptians.

Page 57 – 61

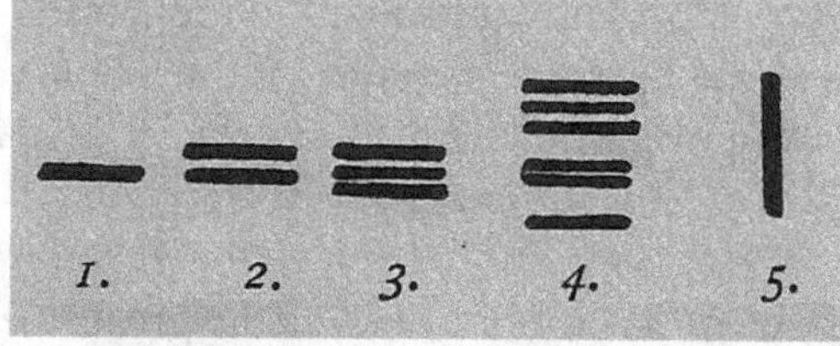

The Uighurs, generally, used a bar or line to express their numerals but quite often reverted to the Naga when inscribing the Mysterious Writing. At times, however, they expressed the Mysterious Writing with their popular form of glyphs. (Figs. 1, 2 and 3.) Sometimes these lines were drawn horizontally, sometimes vertically, apparently dependent on the form of space available. (Figs. 4 and 5.)

THE MYSTERIOUS WRITING AS A KEYSTONE.— Here is an example where we find a combination of the Naga and Uighur forms of numeroals used in a single inscription. The

Keystone (The Mysterious Writing) is the Naga form. The lines are the Uighur form, also the Sun, the symbol of the Deity. I will next show that the Hindu A U M is the same conception as the Mysterious Writing.

CARA OR KARA INSCRIPTION, BRAZIL.— Out on a large prairie-like plain in Northeastern Brazil near the boundary of British Guiana stands an immense rock, having

<skip illustration on top of page 58>

many smooth faces or areas. These smooth faces are literally covered with very ancient inscriptions which are written with the characters of the ancient Karas or Carians. In the neighborhood it is called Inscription Rock.

The following is one of the inscriptions with its deciphering and translation:

A universal symbol as before stated (*Fig. 1.*). The Northern or Uighur form of symbol for writing the numeral one (*Fig. 2.*). Numeral 2 (*Fig. 3.*). Numeral 3 (*Fig. 4.*). Numeral 3 is specialized by not having one end

<skip illustration on page 59>

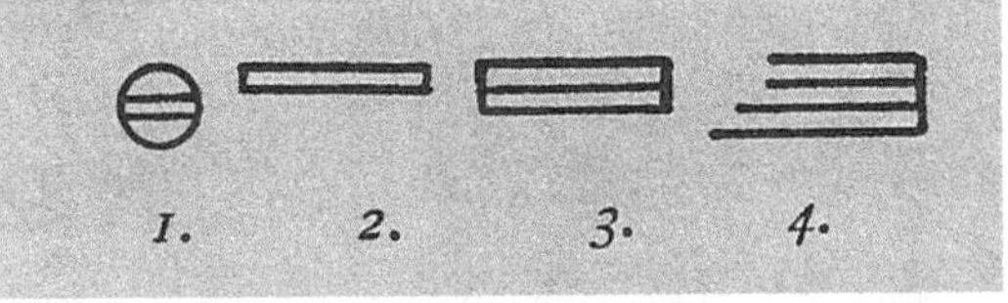

closed. The significance of this will be shown in the deciphering and translation hereafter.

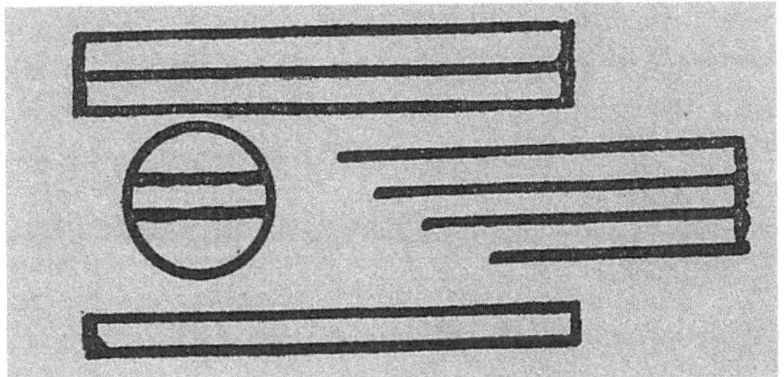

Legend. One became two, two produced three, from these three life was *continued* on.

Continuation is shown in the glyph for numeral 4. In this glyph the bars on one end are not enclosed. The end of a line unattached to anything was the ancient symbol for incompleted, being carried on but unfinished.

I must also note the numeral 1 glyph, a single enclosed bar. A similar bar was used by the Nagas as the glyph for the numeral 5. They made their count in 5's to avoid naming the numeral 10. Ten was the numeral symbol for the Deity, and for this reason was looked upon as being too sacred to use or mention. Thus they made their count two fives for ten, three fives for fifteen, and so on.

TEOTIHUACAN PYRAMID, MEXICO.—On this celebrated pyramid there are many inscriptions. I have selected one in particular for this work.

The first line reads one, two, three, same as the Brazilian writing. The lines or bars here are the pure Uighur. They are not enclosed as with the Carians generally. In the second and third lines the ancient Uighur glyph for man is shown—Mehen.

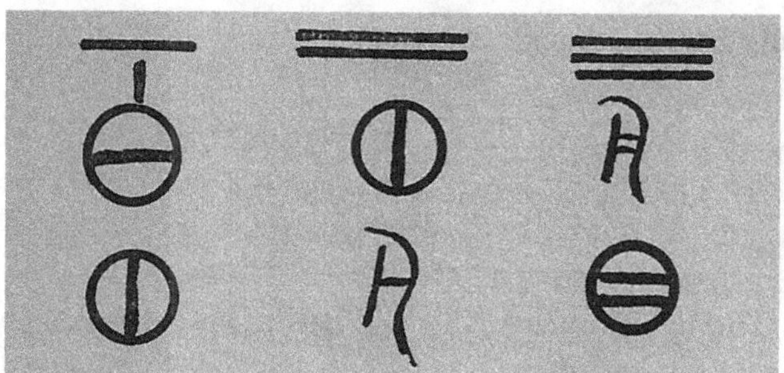

First line one, two, three. Second line Mehen—man is given; having two bars, it says man with the dual principle. In the third line we find one of the bars omitted leaving plain Mehen—Man.

I will now cross the Pacific Ocean from North and South America to China in Eastern Asia.

LAO TSE IN TAO TE KING, A CHINESE BOOK WRITTEN 600 B.C.—"Reason Tao created one. One became two. The two produced three. From these three all mankind descended." Most of the *Tao te King* is made up of extracts from the Uighur copy of the Sacred Inspired Writings of Mu.

Page 64 – 66

Figure I, Group 1. This is the original symbol (See 1.) of the Creator having the dual principle. It is the symbol used in the Sacred Writings of Mu and there called Lahun "all in one" or "both in one." As shown, the glyph

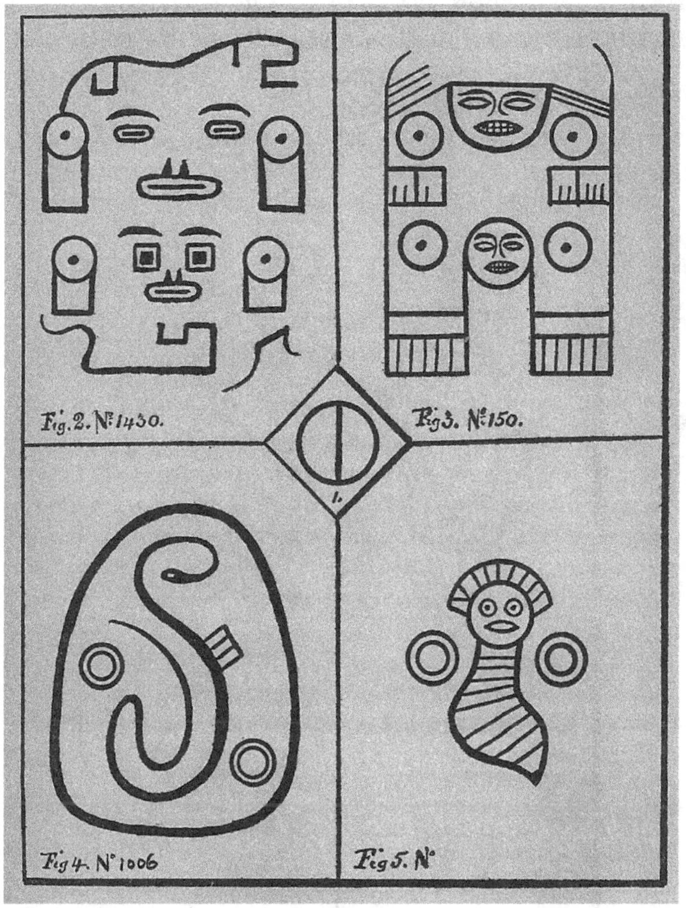

Group 1
A group of tablets symbolizing the Dual Principle of the Creator

is a circle, bisected through the middle by a line. The circle symbolizes the Creator; the two halves, His dual principle. In the ancient Oriental writings the dividing line was drawn vertically by the Nagas and horizontally by the Uighurs. Both, however, have the same meaning. The conception of the Creator having the dual principle was taught tens of thousands of years before these Mexican tablets were written.

Page 67 – 70

. . .

> *Figure 4, Tablet No. 1006.* On this tablet the dual principle is symbolized by a serpent as shown by the two symbols of the Creator. This pattern of the Sun was generally used by the northern people of Mu and the Uighurs.

. . .

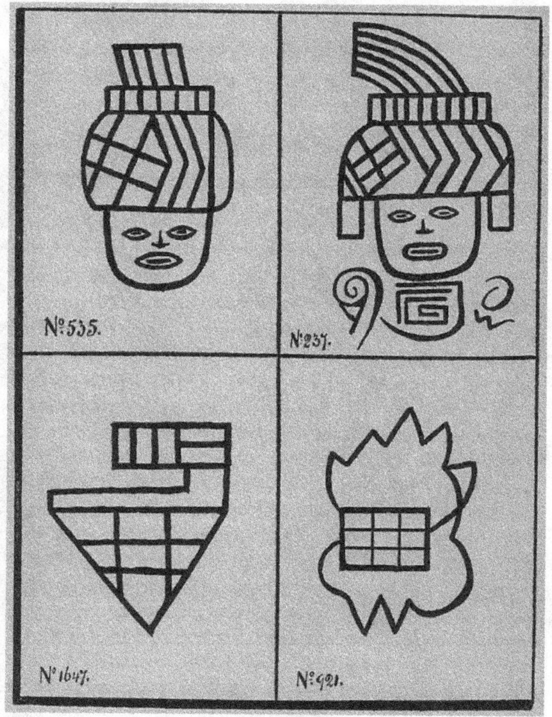

Group 2
The Divisions of Crops and Lands

Both in these tablets and in Oriental writings it is shown that the divisions were not everywhere alike. In the Naga countries, as a rule, one-sixth went for the upkeep of the government and temples. In most of the Uighur districts it was generally one-ninth for the same purposes. Nothing is known as to why these variations in divisions were made. In these tablets I find the variations run from one-sixth to one-twelfth for the government and temples. The division going to the temples is called "The Holy One's Share." In Oriental writings I have found it referred to as "The Lord's Field." In an Oriental tablet where the division in one- ninth, I have found the center square with the symbol of the Creator within it. In fact, it is quite common in the Orient.

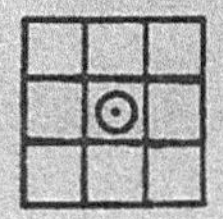

Tablet No. 1647. Shows 9 divisions with the divisions allotted to the government and temples and a common granary for future contingencies.

No. 237. Shows 6 divisions and their distribution. This is the general Naga division and still practiced in some of the small states in India.

No. 921. Shows 9 divisions, the general Uighur percentages.

No. 535. Also shows 9 divisions with their final allotments.

These four tablets are typical of a group of over 100.

Page 75 – 78

Group 5. The Serpent was always the symbol of the waters. From the beginning, Khan, the unadorned serpent, has been the only symbol.

There are at least fifty tablets among Niven's collection symbolizing passages in the 5th Command in Creation as detailed in the Sacred Inspired Writings. I have selected 16 as being typical of them. Since space will not permit of my giving the decipherings of all, I have selected just one, *No. 328.*

Key dissection and deciphering

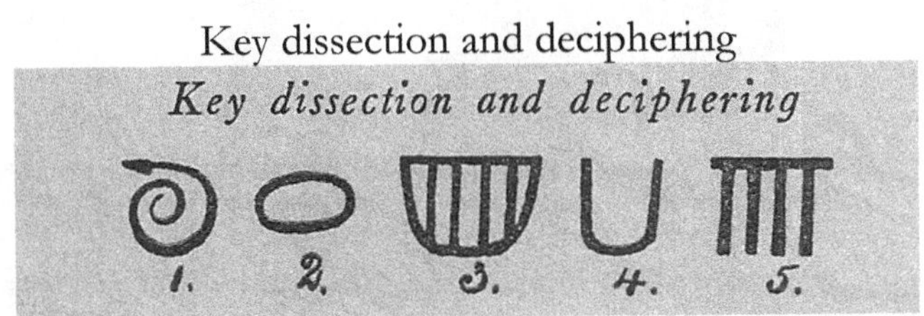

The tableau on this tablet symbolizes the first of nature's lives which appeared in the waters.

Fig. 1. *Khan*, the unadorned Serpent.

Fig. 2. *A Cosmic Egg*, the life germ of today.

Fig. 3. *Compound glyph*, divided in Figs, 4 and 5.

Fig. 4. *An abyss*, a deep hole, depth, etc.

Fig. 5. *The Numeral four*, Uighur form of writing.

The 5th Command in Creation: "And the Creator said, 'Let the waters bring forth life.' Then the arrows of the Sun met the arrows of the earth in the mud of the waters and out of particles of mud formed Cosmic eggs. From these eggs came forth life as commanded."

Only *one* egg is shown in this tablet and that on the *outside* of the coils of the serpent, so that the serpent is shown as being in the act of laying the egg. Being the only egg, it is the first. Therefore, the *first* life to come forth in the waters and *the first life to appear on earth.* In the Sacred Writings, the serpent is shown as having a nest of eggs within her coils, indicating that various forms of nature's lives appeared at the same time.

Below the serpent laying the egg comes the compound glyph. The bottom of the abyss is the ocean's bed. There the mud is settled out of which the cosmic egg is to be formed. The numeral 4 symbolizes the Four Great Primary Forces, the executors of the Creator's commands

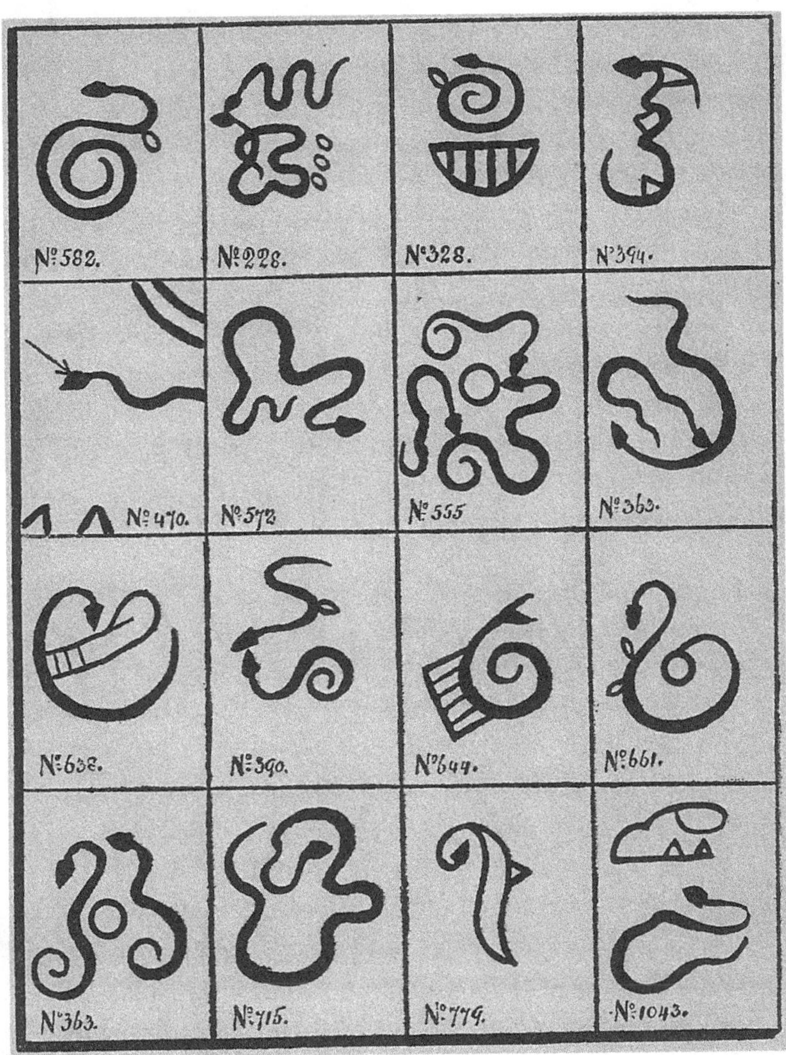

Group 5
The Waters – the Mother of Life.

Legend. "The Creator's command to the Sacred Four was, 'Let the waters bring forth life.' The Sacred Four acted and a cosmic egg was formed out of the mud, the bed of the waters, from which the first of nature's lives on earth came forth as commanded."

This tablet alone is sufficient to show that these old Mexicans obtained their cosmogony from the Sacred Inspired Writings of Mu, the fountain head.

Group 6

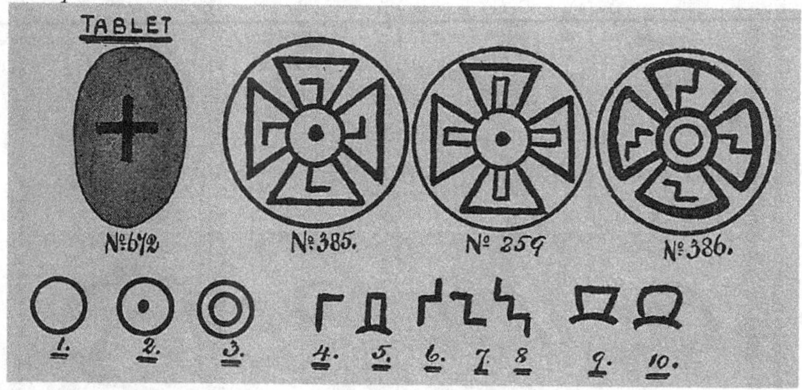

1. The outside circle around the cross: The Universe
2. The Naga collective symbol of the Sun as Ra.
3. The Uighur collective symbol of the Sun as Ra.
4. Glyph which reads: The Builder
5. Glyph which reads: Pillar
6. Glyph which reads: Geometrician
7. Glyph which reads: Architect
8. Glyph which reads: King (Steps to the throne).
9. Glyph which reads: Heaven (triangle).
10. Glyph which reads: Completed.

Chapter VI - ATLANTIS
Page 105

Solon visited Egypt in 600 B.C. Atlantis sank 9000 years before. Add A.D. 2000 plus 9000 plus 600. According to this record Atlantis sank 11,500 years ago, but I shall hereafter show that she did not sink to her present level for a long, long time afterwards. I found in an old Greek record that when Atlantis disappeared there were 3000 Athenian soldiers on her, probably an army of occupation. An Egyptian papyrus states that Poseidon was the first king of Atlantis and that he was followed by a long line of Poseidons, thus forming a Poseidon Dynasty. The crown of Poseidon is shown as having three points, the numeral of the Motherland. His scepter was a trident, again showing Mu to be suzerain. The trident was the form of the Uighur scepter 20,000 years ago and later we find it as the scepter of the Khimers of Cambodia.

Chapter VII - WESTERN EUROPE
Pages 122-124

THE UIGHURS IN EUROPE.—The Uighur Empire was a great colonial empire embodying the whole of Central Asia from the Pacific Ocean to the Ural Mountains with colonies and outposts throughout the central parts of Europe. Only the Atlantic Ocean stopped them from pushing on farther.

There were two migrations of the Uighurs into Europe. The people of the first migration were pretty generally wiped out by the Great Magnetic Cataclysm and subsequent mountain raising. They were not entirely wiped out as three small communities or families were saved. The descendants of these today are: the Bretons of France, the Basques of Spain and the "ginuine Oirish." They are all linguistically related.

Some few years ago a New York contractor undertook some work in Cuba. It was stipulated that local labor should be employed but that supervisors could be brought by the contractor. The contractor accordingly took down his Irish foreman upon whom he could depend. When the party arrived in Cuba they found a group of Basques awaiting them to be used as day laborers. The contractor looked them over; turning to the foreman, he said, "I'll have to get an interpreter. Stay here until I return." Coming back in an hour with an interpreter, he was amused to find his Irish foreman squat in the midst of the Basques enjoying rich jokes. "Send away your interpreter," said Pat. "These people and I spake the same languidge, Gaelic."

A similar story comes from India. Some British soldiers were passing near Nepal on the borders of Tibet, with them an Irish drill-sergeant. Passing through one of the villages the sergeant halted, cocked his ear, then broke ranks and went over to a bunch of squatting natives, exclaiming, "Begorrah! These little divils are talking in me own languidge!"

The *New York Times* of Sunday, August 18, 1929, carried a news item from Leningrad in which it is stated that Professor N. Marr, member of the Russian Academy of Sciences, asserts "that the Irish and Armenians are racial cousins and links them with the Scythians who were among the toughest fighters known to antiquity." He further states that these Asiatic people do not include all of the *present* inhabitants of Ireland, *but only those who are descended from the earliest known dwellers in the Island.*

After the Magnetic Cataclysm, the Biblical "Flood" and the subsequent mountain raising, small companies of Uighurs, called Aryans today, drifted into Eastern Europe from the mountains of Central and Western Asia. This has been noted by Max Müller in his writings. They were descendants of those who had survived the flood and the mountain raising in Asia and Europe. There are Oriental records which speak of both the first and second migrations of Uighurs into Europe. The first entered Europe during the Pliocene, *before* the mountains were raised. The second migration took place during the Pleistocene and *after* the mountain raising, many thousands of years after the first migration. A few remains of the first Uighurs have been found. Probably the most important is the one found a short time ago in what is now Moravia. Here a community had been buried through the flood and mountain raising. The ruins of the entire settlement were found below the foothills of the mountain.

Chapter VII - THE GREEKS
Page 140
Language is one of the great connecting links between various peoples and is more to be depended on than any other form of evidence except written records. The old Greek language was pure Cara-Maya and today has more Maya words in it than any modern language except Cingalese. The Greek alphabet today is pure Cara-Maya. Each letter is either a Maya vocable or a combination of Maya vocables, and forms an epic relating the destruction of Mu, their Motherland and the Motherland of all mankind. It is a phraseological monument to be ever before the eyes of the Greeks to remind them of what befell the forefathers of all men and the Earth's First Great Civilization. Tales of the destruction of the Motherland have been written by the Mayas of Yucatan, the Egyptians, the Hindus, the Chaldeans, the Uighurs and later copied by the Israelites who called it The Garden of Eden in their Biblical legend.

Chapter X - THE WESTERN LINES
Page 169
Without question the most important westerly line from Mu was the northern main line conducted by a people called Uighurs, the forefathers of the Aryan races. The Uighur Empire was possibly

the first, and unquestionably the largest, most important, and most powerful, of all the colonial empires belonging to Mu.

Page 172
"The Naacals, Holy Brothers, teachers of the religion and sciences of the Motherland, left their homes in the Motherland in the East, and first went to Burma and from Burma to India."

The name of the ancient city in the Motherland from which the Nagas sailed was called Hiranypura. The remains of this city are to be seen to this day on one of the Caroline Islands due east from Burma. The first Naga-Maya settlement in Burma was of an exceedingly ancient date. Tablets in the Himalayan monasteries, relating to the first settlement of Uighurs just north of Burma, state that colonization commenced more than 70,000 years ago. The first history that we *know* about Burma commences only a thousand or fifteen hundred years ago, but remains of ancient cities are found in Burma and Valmiki's writings confirm a very ancient date.

Page 205
The Sun was the most sacred because it was the collective or *monotheistic* symbol. The adorned Serpent was the symbol of the Deity *as* the Creator only. As the monotheistic symbol of the Deity, the Sun was called Ra and sometimes written La. When the Sun was spoken of and referred to as the celestial orb it was given its name according to the language of the country. Originally the Sun was pictured as a plain circle. Later the circle was used for other symbolizations such as The Universe, Infinity, etc.; then, to specialize it as the monotheistic symbol, additions were made to it. The Nagas added a dot in the center and the Uighurs, their northern neighbors, a smaller circle instead of a dot.

Page 207
Hindu historians disagree as to the date when the Aryans first came to India. E. G. Tillac says: "The Aryan Invasion of India took place 6000 B.C. to 4000 B.C.," a slight difference of 2000 years. V. A. Smith entirely disagrees with Tillac and says: "The Aryans first commenced to come to India 1500 B.C." For certain reasons hereafter given, I believe that Smith is much nearer right than Tillac.

These Aryans subsequently became known as the Hindu Aryans. The Medes and the Persians commenced to leave their mountain homes in the neighborhood of about 1800 B.C. to 1600 B.C. and completed their exodus about 1500 B.C. The Hindu Aryans were the descendants of a company of Uighurs who were marooned in the mountains of Afghanistan near the Hindu Koosh when the mountains were raised. The Medes and Persians were a continuation of these in the north.

Chapter XIII - THE GREAT UIGHUR EMPIRE
Pages 214-228

The Great Uighur Empire during the Tertiary Era.

The Great Uighur Empire during the Tertiary Era

THE Great Uighur Empire was the largest and most important colonial empire belonging to Mu, *The Empire of the Sun*. Next to Mu herself, the Uighur Empire was the largest empire the world has ever known.

The eastern boundary of the Uighur Empire was the Pacific Ocean. The western boundary was about where Moscow in Russia now stands, with outposts extending through the central parts of Europe to the Atlantic Ocean. The northern boundary is undefined by record but probably extended to the Arctic Ocean in Asia. The southern boundary was Cochin China, Burma, India and a part of Persia.

The history of the Uighurs is the history of the *Aryan races*, for all of the true Aryan races descended from Uighur forefathers. The Uighurs formed chains of settlements across the central parts of Europe back in *Tertiary Times*. After the Empire was destroyed by the great magnetic cataclysm and mountain raising, the surviving remnants of humanity or their descendants again formed settlements in Europe. This was during the *Pleistocene Time*, The Slavs, Teutons, Celts, Irish, Bretons and Basques are all descended from Uighur stock. The Bretons, Basques, and genuine Irish are the descendants of those who came to Europe in *Tertiary Times*. The descendants of those who survived the magnetic cataclysm and mountain raising.

At the time the Uighur Empire was at its peak, the mountains had not been raised and what is now the Gobi Desert was a rich well-watered plain. Here the capital city of the Uighurs was situated, almost due south from Lake Baikal. In 1896 a party of explorers, upon information received in Tibet, visited the site of the ancient city of Khara Khota. They had been told that the Uighur capital city lay under the ruins of Khara Khota. They dug through these ruins and then through a stratum of boulders, gravel and sand fifty feet in thickness, and finally came upon the ruins of the capital city. They unearthed many relics but, their money giving out, they had to abandon their enterprise. They met the Russian archaeologist Kosloff and told him of their find. Subsequently, Kosloff formed an expedition and continued their work at Khara Khota. Kosloff gave a report of his findings which I have already given in *The Lost Continent of Mu*.

Legends all through Oriental countries say: "The whole of Central Asia including the Himalayan Mountains was at one time a flat, cultivated land of fertile fields, forests, lakes and rivers, with magnificently constructed roads and highways connecting the various cities and towns with each other. These were well built cities, huge temples and public institutions, elaborate private houses and palaces of the rulers." Today are to be distinctly seen in the Gobi Desert the dried-up beds of rivers, canals and lakes in those parts of the Desert where the cataclysmic waters did not wash away all the soil down to bare rocks. There are several of these washed-off areas in the Gobi Desert.

Legendary history gives all sorts of conflicting dates as to when the Uighurs were in power. Fortunately, we do not need to rely on legends, for in one of the Tibetian monasteries are some Naacal writings. I quote from one: "The Naacals, 70,000 years ago, brought to the Uighur capital cities copies of the Sacred Inspired Writings of the Motherland." Legendary history states that the Uighurs from the Motherland made their *first* settlement in Asia, somewhere on the coast of the Yellow Sea of today. "From there they extended themselves inland. Their first exodus was to a flat well-watered plain (the Gobi)." After this records are found of them all through Central Asia to the Caspian Sea. Then through Central Europe to the Atlantic Ocean.

Written records tell us that the Uighurs had many large cities. Today these are either washed away or buried under the sands of the Gobi and surrounding lands.

Some Chinese records, bearing a date of 500 B.C., describe the Uighurs as having been "light-haired, blue-eyed people." "The Uighurs were all of a light complexion, milk-white skins, with varying color of eyes and hair. In the north blue eyes and light hair predominated. In the south were found those with dark hair and dark eyes."

I will now consider the following: The cause and date of the destruction of the Uighur capital city.

The cause of the rich, fertile Gobi becoming a desert, and at what period in the earth's history it became a desert of sand and desolation.

An ancient record in a monastery states: "The capital city of the Uighurs with all its people was destroyed by a flood which extended throughout the eastern part of the Empire, destroying all and everything." This ancient record is absolutely corroborated by geological phenomena:

From the roofs of the capital city up to the foundations

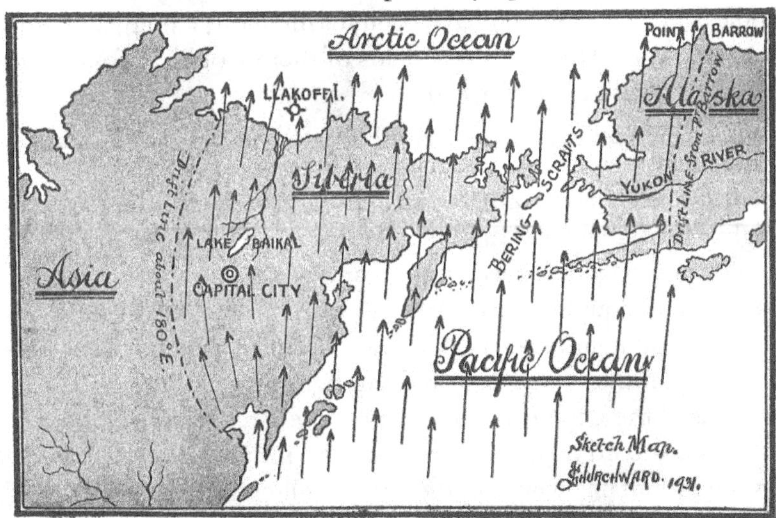

The course of the North Running Wave over Siberia

of ancient Khara Khota the stratum is composed of boulders, gravel and sand, the work of water as acknowledged by all geologists throughout the world. This flood unquestionably was the north running wave of the Last Magnetic Cataclysm, the Biblical "Flood." Back in the 80's I was with an expedition making a geological investigation from a point south of Lake Baikal to the mouth of the Lena River and to the islands beyond in the Arctic Ocean. Our examinations along the route disclosed the fact that some thousands of years before a huge cataclysmic wave of water without ice had passed over this area, traveling from south to north. We found no traces of this flood beyond the 110° East of Greenwich, but we found the evidences of this wave to the limit of our easterly travels. We did not find a single ice marking in any part of Siberia that we covered, that could in any way be connected with this wave. Everywhere the proofs were positive that the wave had passed from south to north. The valley of the Lena appeared to be the main course of the water.

Off from the mouth of the Lena is Llakoff's Island. This island is composed of the bones and tusks of mammoths and other forest animals which had been swept up from the Mongolian and Siberian plains by the flood and carried to this, their final resting place. In these bones we find a confirmation that no ice accompanied the wave, for had there been, their bodies and bones would have been mashed into a pulp, and as in eastern North America, no remains of them would be found and Llakoff's Island never formed.

Geologically this flood occurred at the time that geology claims that there was a glacial period in the Northern Hemisphere. The records tell us that the eastern half of the Uighur Empire, including the capital city and all of the living things on the land, were destroyed and wiped out, but that the western and southwestern parts were left untouched.

Mountains intersect Central Asia in all directions and are especially numerous around and through the parts which comprised the Uighur Empire. Sometime after the flood, I have found no record telling us how long, the mountains were raised. As the mountains went up, the land was literally shaken and torn to pieces by earthquakes when the rocks were raised out of the bowels of the earth, with here and there volcanoes belching out their fiery streams of lava thus adding to the general destruction. How many of the remaining Uighurs, after the flood, survived the destruction caused by the raising of the mountains, cannot be estimated, but very few. This has always been the case in all areas where mountains have been raised in all parts of the earth. The history of a few remnants of the Uighurs that survived, that escaped with their lives in the mountains as they went up, is told in another chapter. The various mountains running through and around the Gobi changed its watersheds. The broken condition of the rocks underneath drained the water from the surface and formed underground rivers. With all water gone from the surface, the Gobi became what we find it today, a sandy, rocky, inhospitable waste. Without question water can be found today within a few feet of the surface in the sandy areas. We found water from 7 to 10 feet below the surface. Legendary history states that the Uighurs extended themselves all through the central parts of Europe. The Book of Manu, an ancient Hindu book, says: "The Uighurs had a settlement on the northern and eastern shores of the Caspian Sea." This was probably the migration spoken of by Max Müller as having taken place during the Pleistocene, the second migration of Uighurs into Europe. It seems to me unquestionable that the early settlers in eastern Europe, as they are called by scientists, were remnants of Uighurs that found their way out from the inhospitable mountains. This seems verified by Max Müller, who wrote: "The first Caucasians were a small company from the mountains of Central Asia." He further states that they came to the Caucasian plains during the Pleistocene, therefore, after the mountains were raised. As before stated, the Uighurs were in Europe before the raising of the mountains. Many of the Central Asiatic tribes today count their time from the raising of the mountains.

In The Lost Continent of Mu I have shown some symbolical pictures photographed by Kosloff at Khara Khota. I also give their decipherings.

TIBET —Tibet lies in Central Asia. It is bounded on the east by China, on the north by Mongolia, on the south by India, and on the west by Kashmir and Turkestan. The Gobi Desert is a part of the northern boundary.

Tibet was once a part of the great Uighur Empire. This was before the mountains were raised. The country then was flat and fertile. Now it is one of the highest plateaus in the world with masses of high mountain ranges, most of which run from a westerly to an easterly direction. In the south is the highest mountain range in the world—the Himalayas. Mount Everest, the world's highest mountain, is in this range and lies within the boundaries of Tibet. Tibet has been called "the roof of the world."

While India has been called "the land of mystery and mysterious sciences," Tibet is her twin sister, if not her rival, in this respect.

In Tibet, in the most inaccessible parts of the mountains, are many monasteries, lamaseries and temples. Shut in from the outside world these monastic orders live their quiet secluded lives, away and aloof from the rest of mankind, unknown to all except a few herdsmen who live in their valleys. Some of the monks in some of these Himalayan and Tibetian monasteries claim that they are the descendants of the Naacals who were driven out of India by the Brahmins about 3000 years ago. These appear to have preserved the Original Religion and some of the Cosmic Sciences of the Earth's First Great Civilization I have emphasized the word "some" because these monasteries out of the hundreds in Tibet can be counted on the fingers of one hand. I know of only three. Most of the monasteries follow a form of Buddhism.

Some years ago Schliemann found in the Old Buddhist Temple at Lhassa a writing relating to the destruction of Mu. This record is a translation from an old tablet written in Pali and Tibetian mixed. The whereabouts of the original is unknown; probably, however, it is lying amongst hundreds of others in one of the rooms of the temple; lying on the floor, dust covered, with a corner or an end peeping through its foul blanket of temple germs.

In the depths of the mountains, on one of the head waters of the Brahmaputra River, are some temples and monasteries. I cannot recollect the exact number now. In one of these monasteries are preserved what is said to be a complete Naacal Library—many thousands of tablets. It was stated to me that this was the Naacal Library which had belonged to the Uighur capital city. They have a weird, legendary history connected with these tablets. I mentioned this fact to my old Rishi and asked him if ever he had heard of them and their weird history. He told me he had in his younger days visited this monastery and was told the history of the tablets. I will repeat it as given to me.

The Legend of the Naacal Library as told by the old Rishi.

"When the great flood swept up over eastern and northeastern Asia, it destroyed the Uighur capital city, drowning all of the inhabitants, and buried a great library which had been brought there by the Naacals from the Motherland. Many years afterwards the Naacals of the west, whom the flood did not reach, went to the ruins of the capital city, dug the tablets out and carried them to a temple in the west. There they remained until the mountains were raised which destroyed the temple and buried them again. Many, many years afterwards the descendants of the Naacals who survived the mountain raising, went and dug them out again and brought them to the temple where they now repose."

Neither this monastery nor the tablets are unknown; they are well known to Oriental scholars. To my own personal knowledge, three Englishmen and two Russians have visited this monastery.

After recounting this legend, I asked the Rishi whether this library was the only complete one in existence. His answer was, "I think not, my son. We have a legend which states that when our Rishi City, Ayhodia, was sacked and burnt by the invading army, the Naacal library was in the secret archives of the temple and never discovered by the enemy. So that if our tradition is correct, buried beneath the ruins of the temple the Naacal library still remains intact, as it has never been dug out."

It has been suggested to me that in my writings I withhold all names of places, routes, passes, etc., in Tibet. Kashmir and Northern India generally, which might be of value in a political sense. The reason given for withholding this information is a perfectly valid one. I feel it my duty and pleasure to comply with the suggestion.

CHINA.—The Chinese civilization is referred to and looked upon as one of the very old ones. As a Chinese civilization it dates back only about 5000 years. It is popularly believed that the Chinese themselves developed their civilization. They did not. The Chinese civilization was inherited from their father's side. Again, the Chinaman is looked upon as a Mongol; he is only half Mongol, his forefathers were white Aryans. During the time of the Uighur Empire, many of the white Uighurs intermarried with yellow Mongols whose country lay to the south of the Uighur Empire, and the descendants of these intermarriages formed the first Chinese Empire. The record reads: "Uighur men married the best of the yellow savages." This without question is a mistranslation, for at the time these marriages were taking place, savagery had never been known on the face of the earth, so that what was meant was unquestionably "the yellow inferior race." This is borne out by traditions which say that "the yellow Mongols were much inferior to the Uighurs, their civilization was below that of the Uighurs." Many of the Chinese today, especially the high class, have quite white skins. This is the Uighur blood showing in their veins. The regular Chinese coolie, the lower classes of the Chinese today, have no Uighur blood in them. They are the descendants of the ancient yellow Mongols. The Uighur parents of these intermarriages were very careful to have their children educated up to the Uighur standard, so that when the Chinese Empire was first formed it was by those having Uighur blood in their veins and educated in the Uighur great civilization. The Chinese civilization, therefore, was the Uighur civilization handed to them by their fathers. There are many writings in the Chinese Tao temples confirming the foregoing and any Chinese scholar can without question confirm it. Another tradition prominent in China is: "The Chinese did not always live in Asia. They came to Asia from a far-off country towards the rising sun."

I have endeavored to find a collection of the numerous Chinese legends in the form of a Chinese Legendary History—it may exist but I have been unable to find it.

I take from *China* by E. H. Parker, page 17, the following:

Name of Dynasty	Number of Rulers	Duration of Dynasty
"Five Monarchs"	Nine	2852-2206 B.C
Hia	Eighteen	2205-1767 B.C
Shang	Twenty-eight	1766-1122 B.C
Chow	Ten	1121-828 B.C.
Chow	Twenty-five	827-225 B.C.

According to this, the average reign in each dynasty was:

"Five Monarchs"	– each reigned 71 7/9 years.
Hia	– each reigned 24 1/3 years
Shang	– each reigned 23 years
Chow	– each reigned 29 8/10 years
Chow	– each reigned 22 22/25 years

Parker says: "The Five Monarchs are altogether mythical. The Hia dynasty is legendary and largely mythical. The Shang dynasty is chiefly legendary. The Ten Chow is semi-historical and the Twenty-five Chow historical."

From the foregoing one must infer that Parker believes only what he sees and nothing that he hears. It would appear that it matters not how true a legend may be, it is a myth unless he sees writings which he can believe in. It has been one of my hobbies to trace myths back to see what they come out of. Ninety times out of a hundred I have found that the myth has its origin in a tradition or legend. The tradition or legend has been so garbled that it has become a perfect myth. It should be remembered that there is no smoke without a fire. I do not doubt for a minute that in many cases what Parker calls myths are really legends slightly garbled. They are traditions only to the people, for behind them in the old Tao temples are to be found written records of the various phenomena.

Parker gives a good and very exhaustive history of China from about 200 B.C. down to present time. He shows the rise and fall of the various Mongol tribes and nations. He is, however, absolutely wrong about the Japanese; and, being wrong about them, other assertions of his are left open to doubt. From his style of writing he would be one to put poor old Marco Polo in prison because he did not bring back a big-horn sheep to show. How Parker accounts for the Gobi ruins and other great prehistoric ruins, I do not know. Apparently, such things mean nothing to him.

Some seven or eight thousand years after the destruction of the Uighur Empire, innumerable little nations came into existence in Eastern Asia. All, apparently, were of the Mongoloid type. The most prominent of these Mongol nations was a Tartar race of which Genghis Khan and Kublai Khan were the principal figures. Kublai Khan lived A. D. 1277, about 600 years ago. Confucius, the great Chinese scholar and philosopher, lived from 551 B. C. down to 480, about 300 years after Chinese history commenced to be recorded in China. The Emperor Che Hwang-te, 214 B.C., ordered all books and literature relating to ancient China to be burnt. A vast amount was seized by him and burnt. Some of the works of Confucius and Mencius were included in this conflagration. It was this king who built the great wall of China to keep back the Heung Noo Tartars from constantly raiding northern China. Che Hwang-te did not succeed in burning all of the ancient writings, for many were saved and hidden in the Tao temples where they are now religiously kept and on no account shown to anyone outside of the priesthood of the temple.

This completes my chapter on Eastern Asia. The next will be on Western Asia. This closes the coffin lid of the Great Uighur Empire as far as Eastern Asia and their capital is concerned.

THE TERTIARY UIGHUR EMPIRE.—When I say the Uighur Empire of the Tertiary Era, I mean the Uighur Empire of 20,000 years ago—before the Magnetic Cataclysm which was the Biblical "Flood," before the mythical geological "Glacial Period," and before the time when the mountains were raised. The map on page 214 is simply a sketch, adapting present land areas to show the extent and size of the Great Uighur Empire. Since 20,000 years ago, many lands have been submerged and many emerged. I have shown a line running across the central parts of Asia and Europe from the Pacific to the Atlantic Ocean. This line is also about the center of the Empire.

Remains of Uighurs have been found in the Balkans. The last western outposts were Ireland, Breton in France and Basque in Spain. How far north in Asia the Empire ran is not known—ancient Uighur cities have been found far into Siberia.

The shaded parts on the map represent questionable boundaries. The only two well-defined boundaries are the Pacific Ocean on the east and the Naga Empire on the south. Whether the Uighurs extended clear across the center of Europe to the Atlantic Ocean or only outposts were established, is a riddle yet unsolved. Today, however, we find their descendants on the Atlantic Coast, whose origins no one has attempted to tell.

In an old Oriental document it is stated that the Uighur Empire was made up of something such as petty kingdoms, principalities or states, each having its own head or ruler yet all forming but one empire under one supreme head or emperor who in turn was under the suzerainty of Mu, the Empire of the Sun. Looking at our own form of government, it is not a difficult proposition to imagine the Uighur Empire to have been an enlarged United States. Mu herself was only the United States of the world.

Chapter XV – Babylonia
Page 237 – 239
THE MEDES AND PERSIANS.—The remnants of the Uighurs which had been marooned in the mountains that were raised along the southwestern parts of the Uighur Empire, come prominently forward upon the historical stage about 8000 or 10,000 years after the destruction of the Uighur Empire. During this eon of time the several little communities grew and waxed strong; when the bleak valleys of the mountains could no longer sustain their growing numbers, they had to find new homes. Then a general exodus took place from the mountains to lower lands where the conditions were favorable to growth and development. This exodus took place from about 2000 B. C. down to about 1500 B. C.

Page 238
Both Medes and Persians were Aryans coming out of the Ah ra ya tribes of the Motherland through the Uighurs. Both Medes and Persians developed into empires from small communities of Uighurs that had been marooned in the mountains. These were survivors of that great Colonial Empire which had stretched her embracing arms from the Pacific Ocean across Asia and into Eastern Europe. In race, language and religion these two peoples

were closely allied. How could it be otherwise, for originally they were the same?

About 600 B.C. we find the Medes grown into a powerful mountain empire. During the early known history of Persia we find her subject to the Medes. Cyrus was the founder of the Persian Empire. He defeated and dethroned Astyages, King of Media, 558 B.C. Then Media in turn passed under the control of Persia.

The Medes and Persians were the last to occupy Babylonia as an Empire. Their appearance in Babylonia gave the death knell to the Semitics there who had been masters of that country for so many thousands of years. Babylon was defeated and embodied into the Persian Empire 538 B. c. The Persian Empire ended 331 B. c. after having been in existence only 227 years. During this time the Persians were on one big jamboree of conquest with a view of subduing the whole world. They had absorbed the western and southwestern parts of Asia, carried their con quests into Egypt and into a small portion of Europe, when their triumphant march was stopped by the Greeks under Alexander the Great. This was the second time in the history of nations that the Greeks stopped empires which attempted to enslave the world. The first was the overthrow of Atlantis 9500 B. C., and the second the overthrow of the Persian aspirations 331 B. c. The Persian flag today carries the emblem of a colonial empire—an emerging Sun on the horizon with rays—thus connecting themselves with the Uighurs and Mu, the Motherland.

Appendix 5: 'Uighur' in the 1931 *Lost Continent of Mu*

Preface –
Page 7
Where the Mexican tablets were written is problematical. They are mostly written in the northern or Uighur symbols and characters. What actual writing there is on both sets is in the alphabet of Mu, the Motherland. Whether they were written in Mexico or in the Motherland and brought to Mexico I cannot say. They are, however, over 12,000 years old as shown by some of the tablets.

Chapter III - THE LAND OF MAN'S ADVENT ON EARTH
Page 65
Niven's Mexican Bird Tablets.
Among Niven's collection of 2600 ancient stone tablets, there are about thirty containing birds. I have selected three as being representative of the whole thirty.

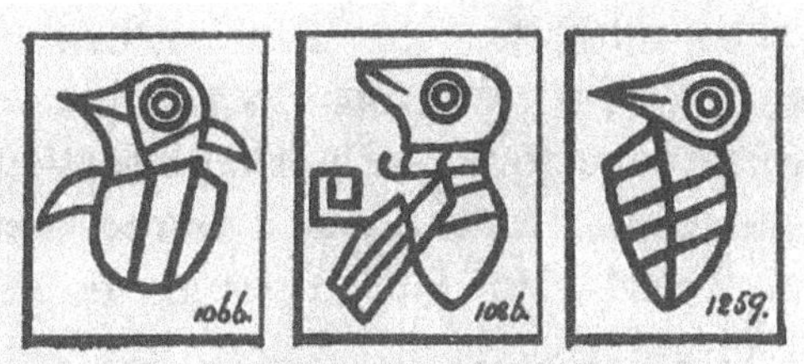

Mexican Bird Tablets

These birds are all symbols of the Creator as told by the writing on them, the old temple esoteric numeral writing. They were drawn by some unknown Uighur people, as the Uighur form of numerals, lines or bars, is used. This is confirmed by the eyes which are the Uighur pattern of the Picture of the Sun and the monotheistic symbol of the Deity.

Page 68
...The most prominent change from the general writings of Mu is in the symbol used by the Indians for symbolizing the waters. In the Naga, Uighur, Karian, American Maya, etc., an unadorned serpent was used, called Khanab, its body generally shown in wavy lines like the rolls of the ocean swell...

Chapter IV - RECORDS OF THE LOST CONTINENT
Page 96 – 97

THE MARQUESAS.—There are several noteworthy ruins on the Marquesan Islands. Apparently no one has ever felt inclined to make an examination of them. I believe the fact that they are there has never before been published.

The foregoing is a long list of Titanic stone remains, and yet I have not enumerated one-half of what are to be found on the South Sea Islands. From this evidence the logical mind can form only one conclusion, and that is: *At one time in the earth's history there was a great continent of land in the Pacific Ocean which embraced all of the groups of islands where prehistoric remains are to be found. This great continent had an exceedingly high civilization.*

That continent was Mu, the Motherland of Man. That her name was Mu and her geographical position are attested by the records of India, Uighur, Egypt, Mayax, Peru and of the cliff dwellers of North America.

These cyclopean remains are her pathetic withered fingers that refused to go down with her broken back and mangled body.

Chapter V - THE EGYPTIAN SACRED VOLUME-BOOK OF THE DEAD
Page 119 – 121

I think the Uighur records will be all that is necessary to convince the most skeptical mind that it is clearly proven by symbols alone that Mu was the Motherland of Man.

The Uighur was the principal colonial empire belonging to Mu at the time of destroyed its eastern half.

The Biblical "Flood," which Chinese legends tell that the Uighurs were at the height of their civilization about 17,000 years ago. This date agrees with geological phenomena.

The Uighur Empire stretched its powerful arms from the Pacific Ocean across Central Asia and into Eastern Europe from the Caspian Sea on. This was before the British Isles became separated from the continent of Europe.

The southern boundary of the Uighur Empire was along the northern boundaries of Cochin China, Burma, India and Persia, and this was before the Himalayas and the other Asiatic mountains were raised.

Their northern boundary extended into Siberia, but how far there is no record to tell. Remains of their cities have been found in the southern parts of Siberia.

Eventually the Uighurs extended themselves into Europe around the western and northern shores of the Caspian Sea, as related in a very ancient Hindu record; from here they continued on through Central Europe to its western boundary, Ireland.

They settled in northern Spain, northern France, and far down into the Balkan region. The late archaeological discoveries in Moravia are Uighur remains, and the evidences on which ethnologists have based their theories that man originated in Asia have been marks left by the advancing Uighurs in Europe.

The history of the Uighurs is the history of the Aryans.

Ethnologists have classed certain white races as Aryans that are not Aryans at all, but belong to a totally different line of colonization.

The capital city of the Uighurs was where the ruins of Khara Khota now stand in the Gobi Desert. At the time of the Uighur Empire the Gobi Desert was an exceedingly fertile area of land.

The Uighurs had reached a high state of civilization and culture; they knew astrology, mining, the textile industries, architecture, mathematics, agriculture, writing, reading, medicine, etc. They were experts in decorative art on silk, metals and wood, and they made statues of gold, silver, bronze and clay; and this was before the history of Egypt commenced.

About one-half of the Uighur Empire was destroyed before Mu went down, the other half subsequent to Mu's submersion.

Professor Kosloff unearthed a tomb 50 feet below the surface at Khara Khota and in it found wonderful treasures, which he photographed, not being allowed to disturb or take anything away. Through the courtesy of the *American Weekly* I have obtained the loan of some of these pictures, two of which I here reproduce with their

Loaned from the Collection of the American Weekly Section of the New York Sunday American

AN UIGHUR QUEEN AND HER CONSORT

An Uighur queen and her consort

SCEPTER CARRIED BY A MONARCH OF THE UIGHURS

Of later date than that shown in the hand of the Queen. Both show the trident

Scepter carried by a monarch of the Uighurs – of later date than that shown in the hand of the Queen. Both show the trident.

decipherings. I think I am safe in believing that these pictures represent a time between 16,000 and 18,000 years ago.

These pictures are symbolical, the various symbols telling who they are, and what they are. In the original they are paintings on silk and represent a queen and her consort in a sitting posture. I will now pick out the symbols of the Queen. On her head is a three-pointed crown with a disc in the center with three sets of rays emanating from it. Behind her body is a large disc, the sun. At the back of her head is a smaller disc, an inferior sun. The large disc symbolizes Mu, the small disc the Uighur Colonial Empire. The crown on her head, a sun with rays on one half only, shows the escutcheon of a colonial empire. In her left hand she carries a scepter, the ends of which are in the form of a trident—three points—the Motherland's numeral.

Her seat is a full-blown sacred lotus, the floral symbol of the Motherland, so that she is depicted as sitting in the lap of and being upheld by Mu, the Motherland. Her consort does not carry a scepter, nor has he a sun with rays, but in its place a sphere. His crown also shows the Motherland's numeral.

Kosloff had pictures of various scepters. This illustration is of a different pattern from the one held in the queen's hand, and of later date, but symbolically reads the same, the ends being divided into three giving the numeral of the Motherland.

Chapter VIII – Man's First Religion
Page 138

The Deity was treated with such reverence that His name was never spoken. The Mayas, Hindus, Uighurs and all other ancients spoke of the Deity as The Nameless. The circle has no beginning nor has it an end. What more perfect symbol could have been devised or selected to teach an uncultured mind the meaning of infinity and everlasting?

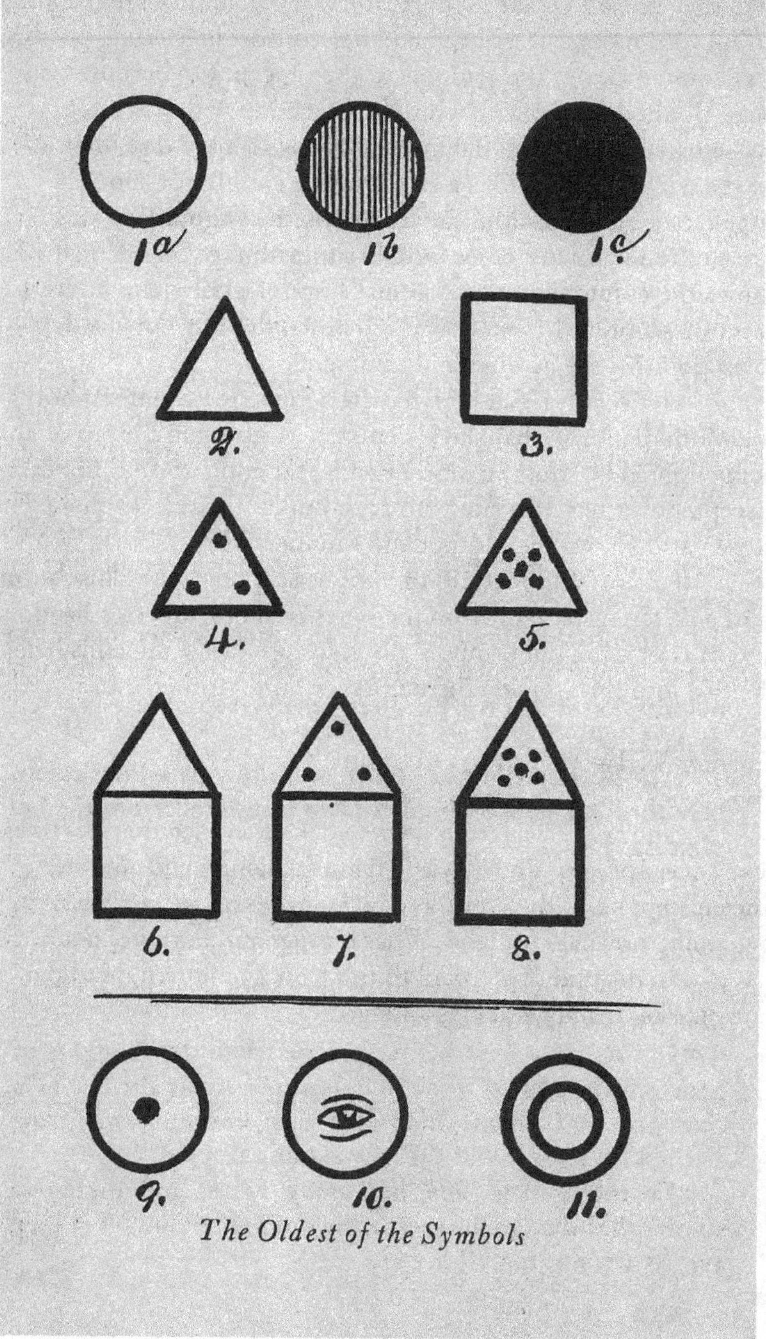

The Oldest of the Symbols

The Oldest of the Symbols

Page 145

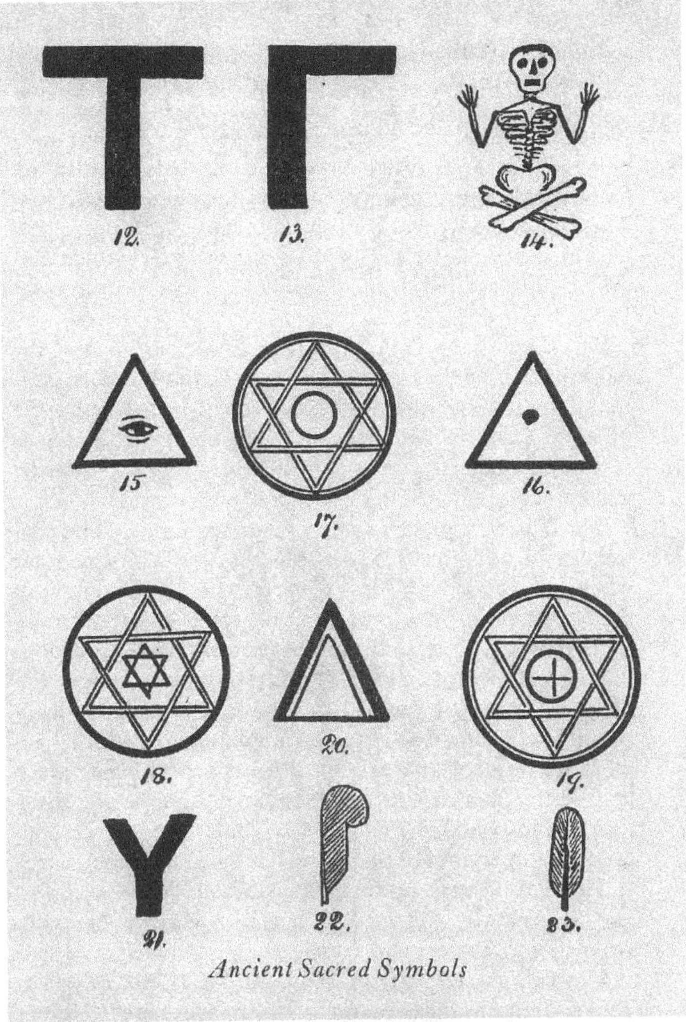

Ancient Sacred Symbols

Page 146(referencing illustration on page 139)

Fig. 11. A circle within a circle was the Uighur or Northern design.

When the Aryans, who were Uighurs, infiltrated into Northern India, they brought with them the Uighur symbols, so that, after many Aryans had settled in India, we find many of the Uighur symbols as common as the Naga. The Sun as the symbol Ra is prominent. The Uighur pattern of the symbol also found its way into Babylonia and into Egypt, carried to these sub-colonies by people from India.

Page 152

The Great Y (page 145). Fig. 21. Taking their learning and religious conceptions from the Uighurs, their forebears on the paternal side, the Chinese replaced the equilateral triangle at the time of Confucius with the figure Y. This they called the "Great Term," the "Great Unite," the "Great Y." "The Y has neither body nor shape, all that has a body and shape was made by that which has no shape. The Great Term or the Great Unite comprehends Three; One is three and three are one."

Page 164

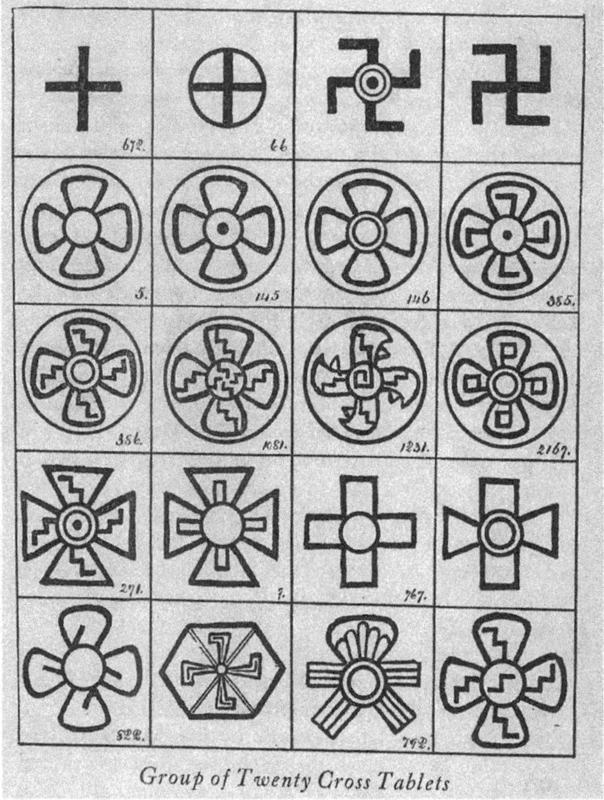

Group of Twenty Cross Tablets

Page 165 – 166

I give here a plate including 20 of Niven's Mexican Stone Tablets with crosses on them: also, the key for their reading.

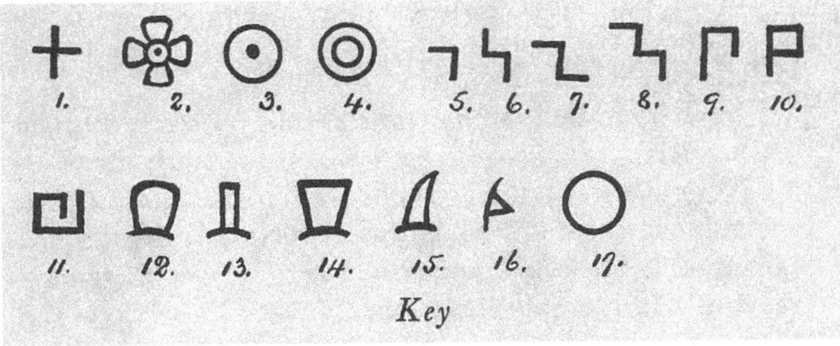

Key

Key for the reading of Cross Symbols.
I. The first original for the Sacred Four. A plain cross.
2. The oldest form of looped cross.
3. Circle with a dot in the center. The Southern or Naga symbol of the Sun as Ra, the monotheistic symbol.
4. A double circle. The Northern or Uighur Symbol of the Sun as Ra. The monotheistic symbol of the Deity.
5. Builder.
6. Architect.
7. Geometrician.
8. The Master Builder.
9. Established, erected.
10. Strength.
11. Hieratic letter H, the alphabetical Symbol of the Sacred Four.
12. Completed. The order has been carried out and has been completed.
13. Pillar.
14. Heaven.
15. A Primary Force.
16. Active. A spear, arrow, javelin or dart.
17. A plain circle around the cross symbolizes the universe, intimating that the forces are working throughout the universe. The circle symbolizing the Universe was called Ul. Ul translated means—the end of space. So that where this circle is used it refers to the end of space, and includes the whole universe.

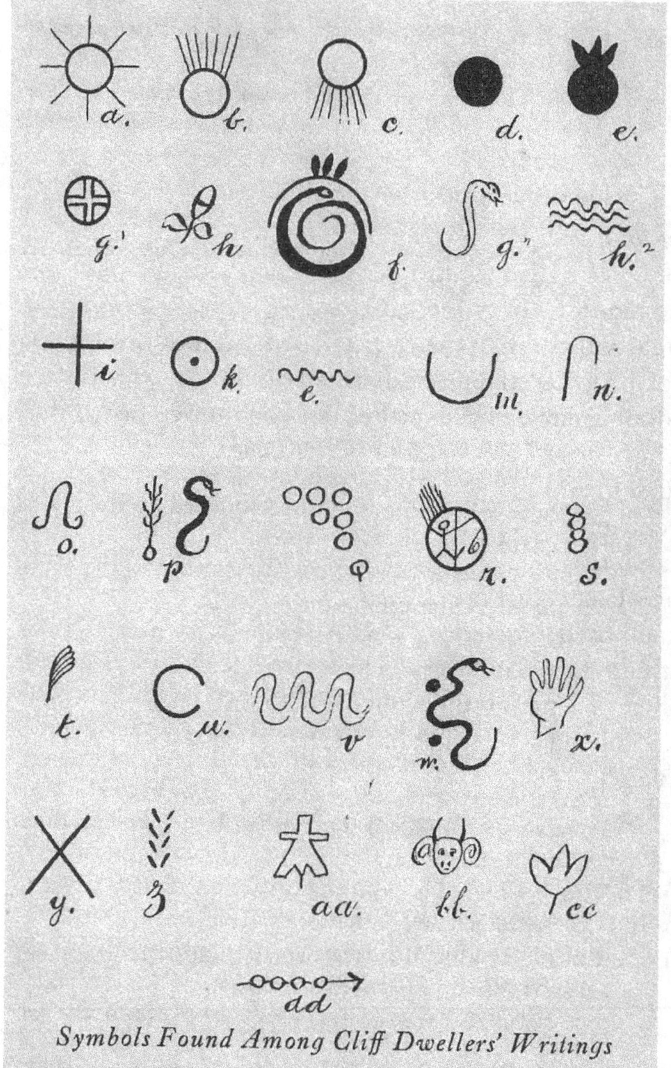

Symbols Found Among Cliff Dwellers' Writings

SYMBOLS FOUND AMONG THE CLIFF-DWELLERS' WRITINGS

(referencing the previous illustration)

R. This is an Uighur-Maya religious symbol.

S. This is the Uighur hieratic letter *h*.

Picture facing page 208

CLIFF DWELLERS' GUIDEPOST

CLIFF DWELLERS' GUIDEPOST

Page 209 (referencing picture facing page 208)
… From the main symbol are shown streams joining each other. The characters on this picture are all Uighur-Maya. These people may have been Mongols….

Chapter XI - NIVEN'S MEXICAN BURIED CITIES
Page 251 – 252

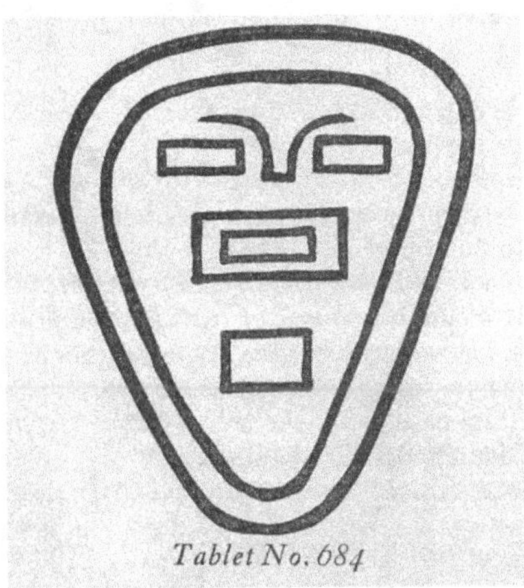

Tablet No. 684

Table No. 684

…

One of Niven's Mexican Stone Tablets. The drawing on this stone is a conventional human face. The outline of the head is made to follow the contour of the stone. It was found by Niven at Hacienda Leon.

It is a wonderful little stone. It talks in the language and writing of Mu, the Motherland, and says "*Mu, the Motherland. The Lands of the West.*" The writing is composed of Naga glyphs only; there is not a single Uighur or Northern character.

Page 253 – 254

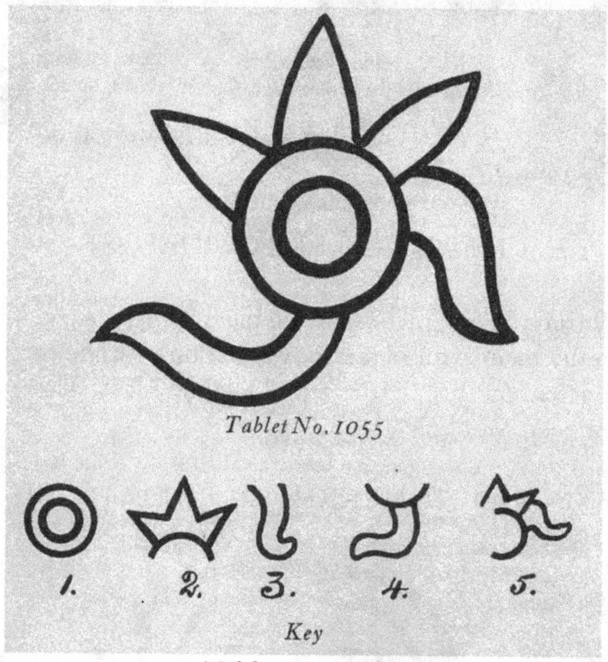

Tablet No. 1055

. . .

No. 1055. Dissection and deciphering. *Fig. I.* This is the Uighur or Northern pattern of the Sun as Ra, the Symbol of the Creator, the Deity.

Fig. 2. This is a three-pointed figure. One of the principal symbols of Mu. Her numeral symbol.

Fig. 3. Is a tongue, the symbol of talk and speech. This tongue projects from Ra: therefore, it is the speech of the Deity.

Fig. 4 This is another tongue but is connected to both Ra and Mu, so it is the Creator, the Deity, that is speaking through Mu.

Legend. The Creator, the Deity speaks through the mouth of Mu.

Page 259 – 260

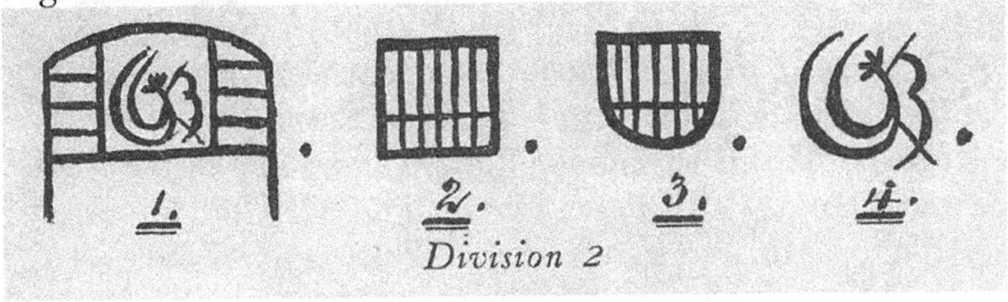

Division 2

. . .

Fig. 4. This is a glyph appearing in the Holy of Holies. It is an Uighur or northern form of writing and reads, "A temple of truth, dedicated to the Sun (the Deity) and under the Jurisdiction of the Motherland."

Chapter IV - THE ORIGIN OF SAVAGERY

Page 290 – 291

These survivors could not return to the plains, for there all was desolation. There was nothing to eat, and so great became their sufferings that they ate one another, and thus, through one of the two geological changes—mountain raising— cannibalism was born into the world. In some instances when the mountains went up, large flat areas were carried up with them, and on this land lived the men and women who had once known all of the luxuries of a great civilization. In time, they lost all knowledge of the higher arts and sciences. They became savages and lived as such.

The most conspicuous instance of this sort was the great Uighur Empire of Central Asia. The eastern half was destroyed by the waters of the Biblical "Flood" and all thereon perished. Afterwards the western half went up, forming the Himalaya and other Central Asiatic mountains. Among these mountains were many plateaus, where the people survived and finally worked their way back into various flat countries. Those of the Uighurs who survived were the forefathers of the Aryan races. In both India and China there are traditions relating to the raising of these mountains, the great loss of life that ensued and the survival of many who lived in the mountains following the great upheaval.

Appendix 6: 'Uighur' in the 1933 *Sacred Symbols of Mu*

Frontispiece:

Courtesy of P/K. Kosloff

The First Man, Dual Principle
Over 20,000 years old. From the ancient Uighur Capital, beneath Kharakhota, Gobi Desert

Chapter III - SYMBOLS OF THE DEITY AND HIS ATTRIBUTES

Pages 69 – 70

No. 1086

Mexican Tablet No. 1086: Those who have read my two books--The Lost Continent of Mu and The Children of Mu will readily see the meaning of two glyphs which I here point out in the bird figure.

The eye of the bird ◎ is the Uighur form of the monotheistic symbol of the Deity.

Projecting from the bird's breast is the hieratic letter H in the alphabet of Mu which was among all ancient people the alphabetical symbol for the Four Great Forces. The body of the bird is in the shape of a pod—symbol for the home of the primary forces. The various lines in connection with the pod are old esoteric Uighur temple writings.

This bird therefore symbolizes the Creative Forces of the Deity and the forces are shown as emanating from or coming out of the Deity. By extension, this figure reads: A symbol of the Almighty showing the four Great Primary Forces coming out of Him.

Pages 72 – 75

THE PYRAMID CROSS. LINE 1.--A group of Crosses among Niven's collection of Mexican tablets is especially interesting. I have called them the Pyramid Crosses because they are designed on the lines of a pyramid. They are the cosmogony of a pyramid illustrated by a cross.

The four arms are composed of four triangles corresponding with the four sides of a pyramid.

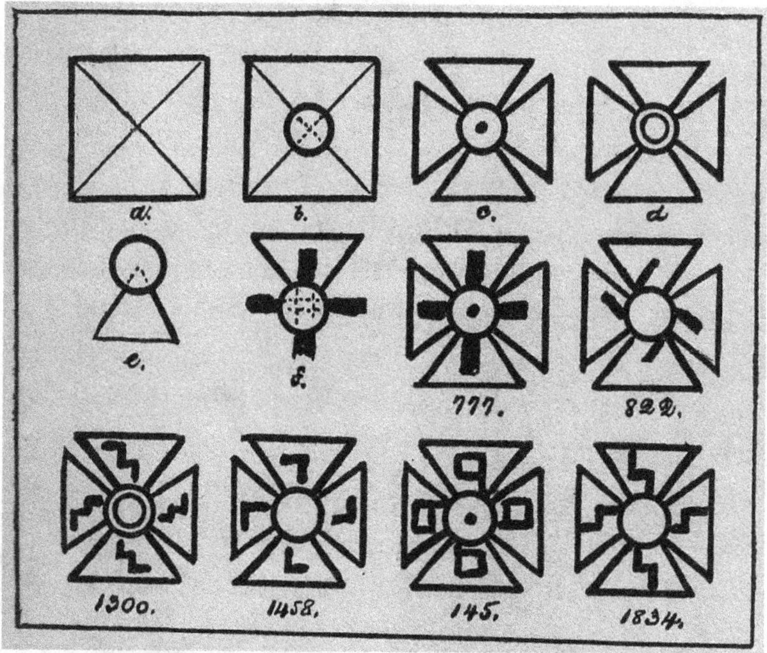

The points of these triangles are covered with the monotheistic symbol of the Deity.

The base of a pyramid is square; the four triangles brought together form a square. The pyramid is built on astronomical lines; so is the Cross.

These Crosses were drawn before the submersion of Mu. Were any pyramids built before that date? I know of none. Were pyramids evolved out of these Crosses?

Fig. A. Is the base of a pyramid divided into four triangles.

Fig. B. Dotted lines within the circle show the points of the triangles, corresponding to the top of a pyramid.

Fig. C. Shows the Cross with the monotheistic symbol of the Deity, Naga Pattern, crowning the points.

Fig. D. Is the same as Fig. C with the exception that the Uighur monotheistic symbol crowns the points.
Fig. E. The point of the triangle covered by the monotheistic symbol. The following is written on these tablets:
"The Four Great Pillars," "The Sacred Four," "The Four Great Architects," "The Four Great Builders" and "The Four Powerful Ones."
No. 777 confirms the fact that the four triangles forming the Cross are the Sacred Four because the symbol within the triangle reads: "Pillar." The four triangles with their inscriptions therefore read: "The Four Great Pillars"--one of the names given to the Sacred Four.
During the life of Mu it was taught that the Four Great Pillars sustained the Universe.
After the destruction of Mu the Universe was forgotten and the earth given the honor of anchoring and sustaining the Pillars. A pillar was placed at each of the Cardinal Points:--North, South, East and West.
THE LOOPED CROSSES. LINE 2.--The evolution of this line started with the plain cross shown in the Sacred Writings and ended with the Deity being added to four loops symbolizing the Four Great Forces, with the names of the Forces given within the loop.

The evolution of the Looped Crosses
The evolution of the Looped Cross

Fig. 1. The Original Cross.
Fig. 2. The oldest form of Looped Cross I have as yet found. It is very ancient from the fact that the symbol of the Deity is of the ancient pattern and not specialized. It is a question in my mind whether a link is not missing between Fig. 1 and Fig. 2; the change appears to me to be too radical for the ancients.
Sometime during the teachings of primitive man trouble apparently began to accumulate over the circle, which was used to symbolize various things. It was then decided to specialize the

circle which symbolized the Deity. The Nagas added a dot in the center and the Uighurs an inner circle. Fig. 2 has neither of these specializations.

Fig. 3^a. Is the same as Fig. 2 except that Fig. 3^a has the Naga pattern of the symbol for the Deity.

Fig. 3^b. Is the same as Fig. 2 except that this cross has the Uighur pattern for the symbol of the Deity.

Fig. 4. This figure shows the last addition to the Looped Crosses. Within the arms of the loops the names of the Force are written, in this case the name of the Force being "builder" (a two-sided square).

Pages 80 – 81

TRUNCATED FIGURES.--Among the Mexican Tablets--Niven's collection--I find over one hundred peculiar truncated figures.. They are purely conventional and were not intended to represent any of Nature's lives.

On deciphering them I found that they are symbolical of the workings of two of the Great Primary Forces.

The trunk indicates the direction in which these Forces work.

The body is that of a chrysalis or pod, the symbol for the home of the Primary Forces. The lines are the numeral writings of the ancients--Uighur pattern.

The legs and arms point to the positions of these Forces under certain conditions.

Truncated Figures
From Niven's collection of Mexican prehistoric tablets

Truncated Figures
From Niven's collection of prehistoric tablets

Chapter IV – The Creation
Pages 104 – 105

UIGHUR.--The frontispiece of this book, coming from the ancient capital of the Uighurs destroyed about 18,000 to 20,000 years ago--Chinese records say 19,000 years ago--is probably the oldest record of man being created with the dual principle.

There are in this world those, the spiritual part of whose brains are so finely keyed to each other, that words are unnecessary to express the feelings of one towards the other when they *first* meet. These possibly are the two halves of man and woman which in bygone times made one soul. All the past is bridged at a glance. The divine, pure love for one another leaps into life again on the instant. Many modern writers have vulgarly termed this "the man call." It is not the man call; it is the souls' call, mates. The "man call" is materialism. Materialism has nothing to do with it, because the call is spiritual.

Again, two persons, meeting for the first time, may or may not take a dislike to one another. One of them at least may take a dislike to the other and mistrust the other for no apparent reason. This is popularly termed "first impressions." Probably if their past incarnations could be recalled and they could see all that happened in them, the question would be answered.

A glyph, generally a circle but sometimes oblong with two parallel lines drawn through its center dividing it into three parts as shown Cut. 1 (Niven's Mexican Tablet No. 2379), is a common universal symbol.

It is found among the cliff writings of our western states, in inscriptions on the Mexican Pyramid at Xochicalco, in the Maya writings of Yucatan. It appears in a writing on Inscription Rock, northeast Brazil

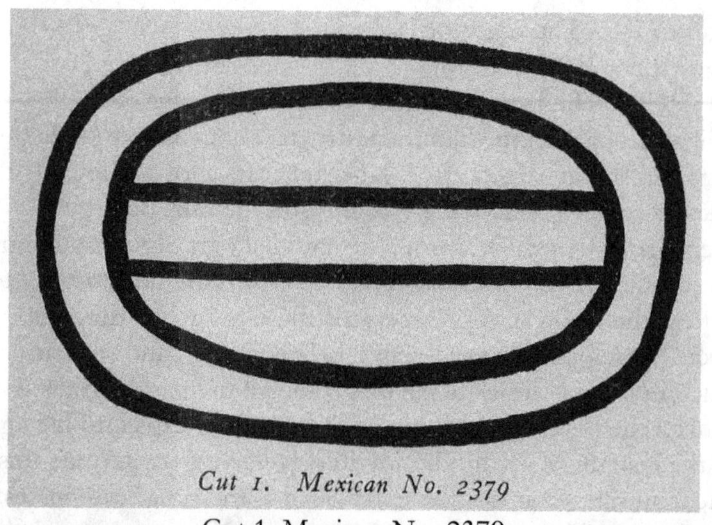

Cut 1. Mexican No. 2379

Cut 2. A paragraph in the Sacred Inspired Writings
(Naacal Writing)

near the boundary of British Guiana, and in other various American carvings. It occurs in the ancient writings of the Uighurs, Hindus, Babylonians and Egyptians.

Pages 107 – 110
THE MYSTERIOUS WRITING.--The Mysterious Writing consisted of either six small circles or six small disks, placed so as to form a triangle, pyramid or keystone. The rows are so placed that they count-one, two, three.

Cut 3.
The Mysterious Writing

The two figures forming Cut 3 are written with the Naga form of numerals. Sometimes the Nagas used circles, at other times disks; this appears to have been optional, dependent on the taste of the writer.

The Uighurs, generally, used a bar or line to express their numerals. I find their expression of the one, two and three most frequently written thus — = ≡ or | || |||.

KARA INSCRIPTION IN BRAZIL.--On a large prairie-like plain in the northeastern part of Brazil near the boundary of British Guiana stands an immense rock with many smooth faces which are literally covered with very old inscriptions in the characters of the ancient Karas or Carians.

The following is one of the inscriptions with its deciphering and translation:

1. This is a universal symbol found in the writings of all ancient people.
2. The Northern or Uighur form of writing the numeral 1. (Cara or Karian pattern)
3. Numeral 2.
4. Numeral 3. This glyph is specialized by not having one end closed which gives it a special significance.

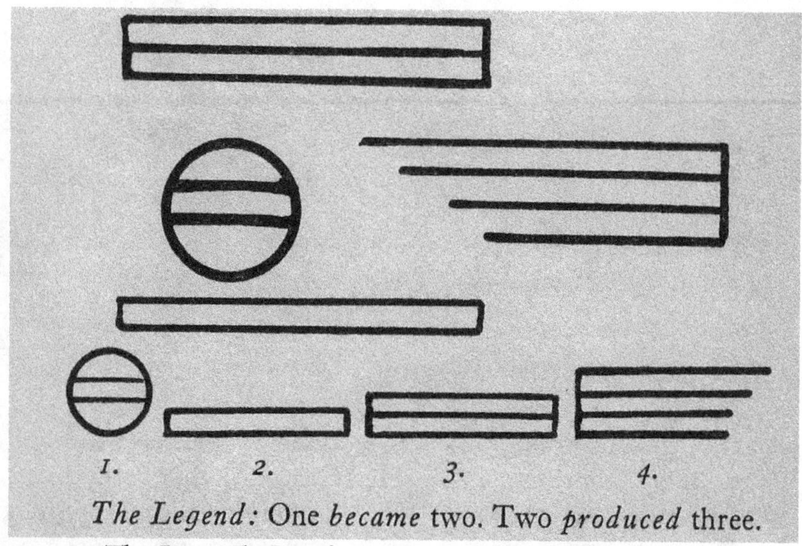

The Legend: One *became* two. Two *produced* three.

The Legend: One *became* two, Two *produced* Three.

The Legend: One *became* two. Two *produced* three. From these three the life was *continued* on.

The continuation is shown in the glyph for numeral 3 where the ends of the bars are left open. The ancients designated by unattached ends that unfinished work was being carried on.

It may be well to note here that the Cara glyph for 1, an enclosed bar, was the Naga glyph for 5. All Naga counts were made up of 5's; thus ten would be two or twice five. Ten being the numeral symbol of the Infinite, was never used. As the symbol of the Infinite it was looked upon as being too sacred.

I have here shown a South American inscription composed of a symbol or vignette with its meaning given in script. This, to a great extent, follows the character of the Sacred Inspired Writings of Mu; further, it is unquestionable that this passage was taken from the Sacred Writings for on the other side of the world comes the Motherland. In China we find Lao Tzu in *Tao te King*, using virtually the same words about 600 B. C. which he took from the Sacred Writings of the Motherland.

XOCICALCO PYRAMID--MEXICO.--On this celebrated pyramid there are many inscriptions. I have selected one which appears to me to be relative to the creation of the first pair.

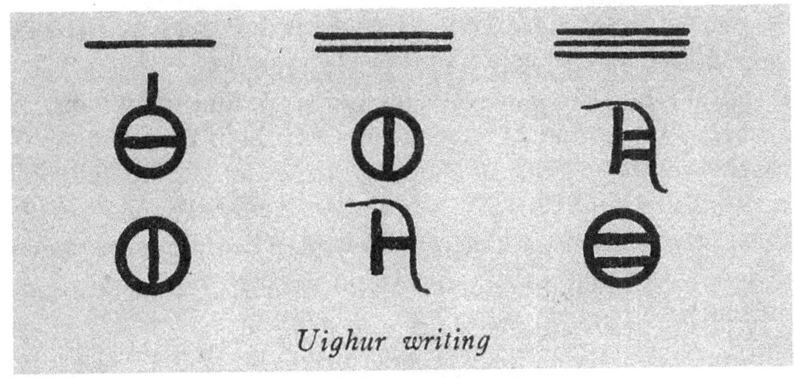
Uighur writing

Uighur writing

1st Line. Numerals one, two and three with their hidden meaning as previously given.

2nd Line. Includes the Uighur glyph for man having the dual principle. Man before he became divided.

3rd Line. Includes man as the male principle only

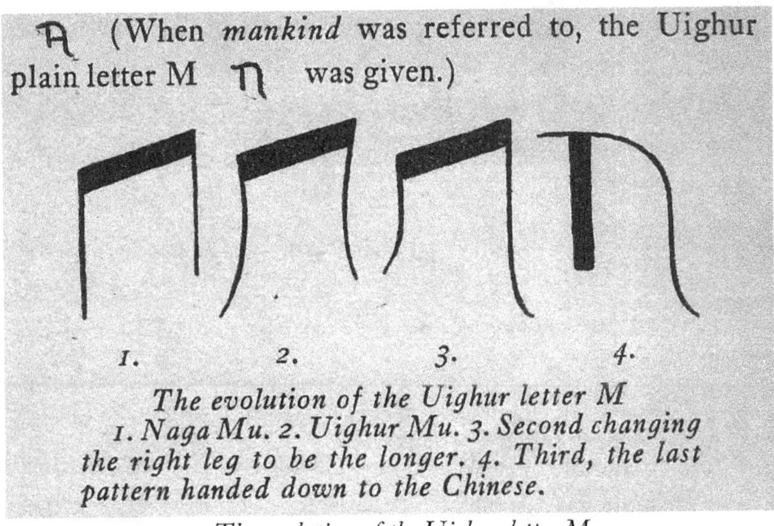
(When *mankind* was referred to, the Uighur plain letter M was given.)
1. 2. 3. 4.
The evolution of the Uighur letter M
1. Naga Mu. 2. Uighur Mu. 3. Second changing the right leg to be the longer. 4. Third, the last pattern handed down to the Chinese.

The evolution of the Uighur letter M

1, Naga Mu. 2. Uighur Mu. 3. Second changing the right leg to be the longer. 4. Third, the last pattern handed down to the Chinese.

Chapter V – SYMBOLS USED IN RELIGIOUS TEACHINGS
Page 119
THE CIRCLE.--The Circle is a picture of the Sun and was the symbol of the Infinite One. As it embraced all of His attributes it was the Monotheistic Symbol. Being the Monotheistic Symbol it was considered the Most Sacred Symbol of all. According to legend, the Sun was selected for this symbol because it was the most powerful object that came within the sight and understanding of man at that time.
The circle having no beginning and no ending also symbolized:--everlasting, without end and infinity.
Before very long it is shown that the circle was being used to symbolize so many things that it became necessary to specialize the circle when using it as the Monotheistic Symbol of the Deity. The Nagas made an addition by placing a dot in the center of the circle. The Uighurs added a smaller circle within, making it a double circle.

Page 121-123

Fig. 1. The Original Monotheistic Symbol of The Deity.
Fig. 2. A subsequent change made by the Nagas.

<skip illustration on page 122>

Fig. 3. A subsequent change made by the Uighurs.
Fig. 4. Part of the headdress of some of the Egyptian gods.
Fig. 5. This generally appears as a red sphere on tops of pillars and monuments to the dead.

Page 146 – 147

Temple Porch with Two Pillars

Temple Porch with Two Pillars

Temple Porch with two Pillars: Niven's Mexican Stone Tablet No. 50, over 12,000 years old.

This temple has a dedication over the center of the arch, the hieratic letter H in the alphabet of Mu. This was the alphabetical symbol of the Four Creative Forces. So this temple was dedicated to the Four Great Primary Forces. Below are shown two pillars, each one has four sections the numeral four (Uighur form) corresponding to the four Primary Forces. The left hand pillar is capped with the glyph strength, and the right hand one with the glyph establish.

The ground plan of this temple which is on another tablet shows the left hand pillar to be square and the right hand one round.

A very old written record, dating back to about 11,000 years, comes from the Greek, and refers to the pillars of the temple dedicated to Poseidon of Atlantis.

The foregoing I think clearly establishes the antiquity of pillars as sacred symbols, with their shapes and meanings.

Pages 155 – 156

[…]THE ROADWAY OF THE SOUL.--I have found in my wanderings two figures prominently placed, but never came across the name by which they are called. As they are generally found on the outside of, and on the walls and ceilings of, burial chambers, I have given them the name as shown in the above caption. Some day perhaps their correct name may be known, then this temporary name can be abandoned.

For many years the spiral figure, shown in cut, has

Facing Page 155

Courtesy of Mrs. M.V.L. Hudson

The Roadway of the Soul

been a puzzle to me, as it has been found all along the line of the great Uighur migration. The picture I am showing comes from New Grange, County Meath, Ireland.

The figure is either an explanation of the esoteric or hidden meaning of the hieratic letter N in Mu's alphabet, or the letter itself, highly embellished, I cannot say which. After a careful study of many of the writings of Mu in which the letter N appears, I find a slight variation in them. Sometimes they are formed thus ᔐ, sometimes thus ᔐ. The difference is that in one the ends are left open—in the other they are closed—there are no ends. As there are no ends, the figure becomes a continuous line, returning to the starting point, and proceeding on as it can find no place to stop. It is therefore equivalent to a circle, which has no beginning or end.

In the picture shown from New Grange it will be seen the spirals have no ends, but when the center is reached the line returns on itself. There is no starting point in either of the spirals and no end given, consequently, these spirals are also the equivalent of a circle.

Page 157

On the walls of New Grange there are carved other symbols, spirals, squares, zig-zags, et cetera.

@ A spiral with an end pointing to the right is an ancient Uighur symbol meaning, "going to somewhere." It is also found in Mexico and among the North American Indians.

Page 158

▼ Is the Uighur mountain and Chinese Yo; it is equivalent to the triangle. Freely read, "ascended."

Page 161 – 163

THE SACRED SEVEN.--The original sacred Seven was the Seven Great Commands of the Creator. These were given to the Four Great Primary Forces, to carry out "his will, command or wishes," thus emanating from the Creator. They are the Creative Forces of the Almighty.

The predilection of ancient peoples in their sacred ceremonies for the use of the numeral Seven is very great and conspicuous.

Chaldeans: The Seven Days of rainfall that produced the "Flood."

Hindu: The Seven Days of the prophecy of the Flood made by Vishnu to Satyravata.

The Bible: The Seven Days of the prophecy of the Flood made by the Lord to Noah.

Babylonian: The Seven Vases used by the priests in their sacrifices.

Persian: The Seven Horses of the Aryans, that drew the chariot of the Sun. The Seven Apris or shapes of the flame. The Seven Rays of Agni.

Hindu: The Seven Steps of Buddha at his birth. The Seven Rishi Cities of India.

Egyptian: Their Seven Days of Creation. Their Seven Days of the week. And the Seven Classes of Egyptians.

Greek: The Seven Islands sacred to Proserpine. The Seven-headed Hydra killed by Hercules.

Norse: The Seven Families who accompanied the mythical Wotan, founder of the city of Nachan.

Hebrew: The Seven Lamps of the Ark. The Seven Branches of the Golden Candlestick. The Seven Days' Feast of the dedication. The Seven Years of plenty. And the Seven Years of famine. The Seven People who escaped from the flood.

Christians: The Seven Golden Candlesticks. The Seven Churches with the Seven Angels at their head. The Seven Heads of the beasts that rose from the sea. The Seven Seals of the Book. The Seven Trumpets of the angels. The Seven Vials of the wrath of God. The Seven Last Plagues of the Apocalypse.

Nahualts: The Seven Caves from which the ancestors of the Nahualts emerged.

Zuni Indians: The Seven Cities of Cibola.

Uighurs: The Seven Sacred cities of the Uighurs.

Atlantis: The Seven Great Cities of Atlantis.

Carian: The Seven Antilles.

Marquesan: The Seven People who were saved from the "Flood."

The Seven Marouts or genii of the winds in the hierarchy of Mazdeism.

The Seven Rounds of the ladder in the cave of Mirtha.

Mu, the Motherland: The Seven Sacred Cities with their golden gates.

Chapter VI – SYMBOLS RELATING TO MU
Page 186

Another glyph symbolizing the Sacred Four. This was a very favorite symbol among the Uighurs and is revered by the Chinese today. I have also found it as a dress ornamentation among the South Sea Islanders especially the Polynesians.

Chapter VII – SACRED SYMBOLS CONNECTING NORTH AMERICA TO MU
Page 204

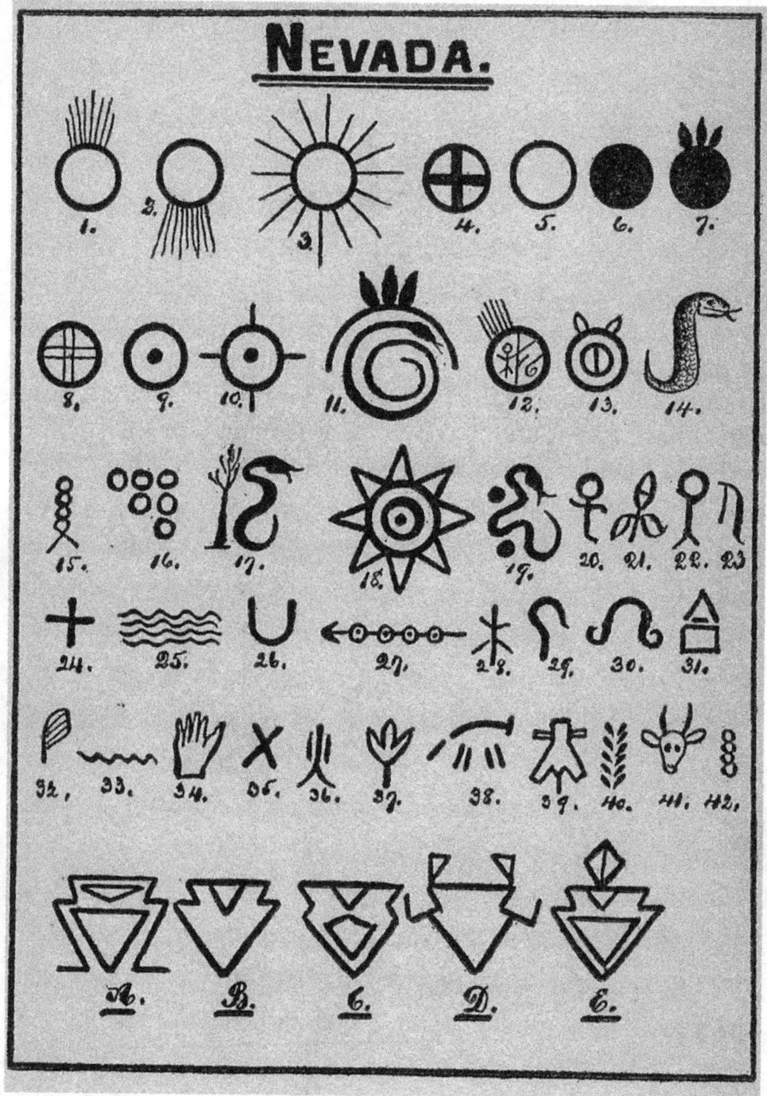

Page 207

[…]

22. An Uighur Symbol. Gone down from the sight of the sun.
23. An Uighur symbol, Mehen--Man.

[…]

Page 208

[…]

28. An Uighur symbol. I cannot give the meaning.
29. An Uighur symbol, the letter X.
30. An Uighur symbol for hard.
31. An Uighur symbol, heaven above earth.
32. An Uighur pattern of the feather, symbol for Truth. Universal throughout the world.
33. One of the glyphs for the letter N in the alphabet of the Motherland.
34. A human hand, not a symbol.
35. The ancient symbol for the active and passive elements in nature. Universal throughout the world.
36. An Uighur symbol, fires of the underneath.
37. An Uighur pattern of the symbol for multitudes. The Egyptians reversed the leaf, having the stem on top.

[…]

Page 209

[…]

There are two distinct eras of writings, written by neither Naga, Uighur nor Yucatan Maya, probably one or two of the ten tribes of the Motherland, who were in close proximity with all three in the Motherland.

[…]

Page 214 – 215

[…]

One of the most extraordinary picture writings I have ever come across is a painted tableau depicting the submersion of Mu, and one of two pictures--only that I have found depicting the submersion of Mu. The other is the Egyptian. The picture has three archaeological divisions:--*Top*--A serpent with a plume of feathers on its head. *Middle*--The Thunder Bird with its talons embedded in the body of the Killer Whale. *Bottom*—The Killer Whale covered with symbols. This tableau comes from the Nootka Indians who live on the west coast of Vancouver Island, British Columbia, Canada.

[…]

Page 216 – 217

Bottom. The Killer Whale. This division is the crux of the whole picture--the top and middle amounts to but a preliminary setting. The Killer Whale is purely a conventional fish, just a symbol. The eye is made out of the compound symbol mother and land which, conjoined, reads Motherland. The pupil is a solid black square symbolizing darkness, therefore the Motherland is in darkness. The neck is shown as broken, with the symbol, abyss and magnetic Forces, falling from the wings of the Thunder Bird (the Four Great Forces) into the broken neck, thus showing that it is subsidiary forces coming from the Primary that is accomplishing the destruction '

Within the mouth is the symbol for flowing water, at the end of the mouth a passageway is shown, beyond this passage way is the hieratic letter U, the alphabetical symbol for an abyss, thus saying the Motherland has been carried down into an abyss of water. Directly following the abyss is the Uighur numeral four, four bars. On the backbone is the Naga form of number four, four circles or disks. The number four was the numeral symbol for the Four Great Primary Forces. Above the backbone are five bars, the Uighur way of writing five. Five was the numeral symbol of the full or monotheistic godhead.

Legend. Thus repeating within the fish what was said by top and middle figures. The whole as a legend would read: the Creator ordered or commanded the submergence of Mu. His executors the Four Primary Forces proceeded to carry out the command by dispatching subsidiary Forces to do the work. These caused the land to sink and the waters to cover over the sunken land.

Chapter IX – RELIGION IN EGYPT AND INDIA

Page 274 – 275

THE RELIGION OF INDIA.--The religion of very ancient India was that of the Motherland, brought there from Mu by the Naacals, a holy brotherhood. These men were taught religion and the Cosmic Sciences in the Motherland and when proficient were sent to the colonial empires to form colleges and perfect the local priesthoods, who in turn taught the people.

About 5,000 years ago, a race of Aryans began to drift down into India from the bleak valleys of the Hindu Koosh and adjoining mountains. Their first settlement was among the Nagas in the Saraswatte Valley. They were just hardy mountaineers, uncouth and uneducated. The Nagas, the most highly educated race in the world, took compassion on them, welcomed them into their schools and colleges, educated and advanced them. The Nagas received them too well for their own good, for, it called from the mountains nearly all who had multiplied there since the destruction of the great Uighur Empire of whom they were descendants. In time these Aryans dominated the whole of the Northern parts of India including their schools and colleges. Thinking they had learnt from the Naacals all there THE RELIGION OF INDIA.--The religion of very ancient India was that of the Motherland, brought there from Mu by the Naacals, a holy brotherhood. These men were taught religion and the Cosmic Sciences in the Motherland and when proficient were sent to the colonial empires to form colleges and perfect the local priesthoods, who in turn taught the people.

About 5,000 years ago, a race of Aryans began to drift down into India from the bleak valleys of the Hindu Koosh and adjoining mountains. Their first settlement was among the Nagas in the Saraswatte Valley. They were just hardy mountaineers, uncouth and uneducated. The Nagas, the most highly educated race in the world, took compassion on them, welcomed them into their schools and colleges, educated and advanced them. The Nagas received them too well for their own good, for, it called from the mountains nearly all who had multiplied there since the destruction of the great Uighur Empire of whom they were descendants. In time these Aryans dominated the whole of the Northern parts of India including their schools and colleges. Thinking they had learnt from the Naacals all there was to be learnt, they proceeded to drive their gentle, kindly instructors out of the country into the snowcapped mountains of the North.

Chapter X – THE TWIN SISTERS--RELIGION AND SCIENCE

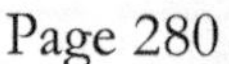

Page 280

Courtesy of George N. Leiper.

One of the two oldest known bronzes in the world—a symbolical figure of Mu as the mistress and ruler of the whole earth. It was made in either Mu or in the Uighur Capital City over 20,000 years ago.

One of the two oldest known bronzes in the world. It is a symbolical figure of Mu as the mistress and ruler of the whole earth. It was made in either Mu or in the Uighur Capital City over 18,000 years ago.

Courtesy of George N. Leiper

Appendix 7: 'Uighur' in the 1934 *Cosmic Forces of Mu Vol. 1*

Chapter 1 – Origin of the Great Forces
Page 26 – 27
MEXICAN TABLET NO. 1086. A CONVENTIONAL BIRD.
I am using this tablet to confirm the previous one, inasmuch as I claim that the primary forces originate directly from the Creator. In all parts of the earth, among all ancient peoples, birds were one of the symbols for the creative forces. In America it was and is called the "Thunder Bird." In the "Lost Continent of Mu" Indian legends and their beliefs about the 'Thunder Bird" are given. I will now confirm Tablet No. 1086 regarding the origin of forces. The eye of this bird is a double, which was the Uighur symbol for the Deity or Creator. The Hieratic letter H — the alphabetical symbol for the four great primary forces — the sacred four. This is shown projecting from the body, therefore projecting or coming out of the Creator Himself. Beneath the letter H is an apron composed of four bars. Four was the numeral symbol for the sacred four.

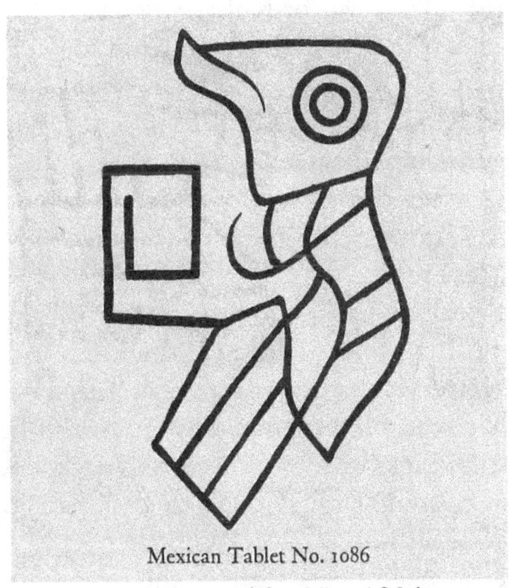
Mexican Tablet No. 1086

Mexican Tablet No. 1086

Appendix 8: "Khara Khota – Kosloff"

Khara Khota
Kosloff.
Moscow.
One of the most picturesque and important of archaeological discoveries of the century has been made by Professor P. K. Kozloff, of Moscow, under the sand-covered ruins of Khara Khoto, in the Gobi Desert of Mongolia.
Khara Khoto, or the Black City, was the capital both of Genghis Khan and Kubla Khan, two of the great Mongol conquerors, who during their lives swept with their hordes over Asia and a good part of Europe. It was of Kubla Khan that the English poet, Coleridge, wrote that strange and haunting verse of his, beginning:
"In Xanadu did Kubla Khan
A stately pleasure-dome decree
Where Alph, the sacred river, ran
Through caverns, measureless to man
Down to a sunless sea."
Digging down through half-a-hundred feet of shifting sand, Professor Kozloff has unearthed there the tombs of what appear to be the legendary Seven Kings of ancient Tartary - certainly the oldest kings that ever ruled any civilization. At this depth the tools of his men struck brick and fossilized black wood. Cutting through this an opening large enough to let a man go through, they lowered Kozloff into the black depths.
As the explorer reached the bottom of the secret chamber his flash revealed one of the most astonishing sites ever seen by an archaeologist - stranger than the scene that met the eyes of the finders of old Pharaoh Tutankhamen's tomb.

He was in a great vaulted chamber. In the center of the chamber was a long table of fossilized wood.
And on seven thrones, each facing the west, sat seven mummies, each dressed in gorgeous robes and with heavy gold masks over their faces. On the table were large bowls of jade, whose cups showed that they had once held some crimson liquid. Another bowl was at the feet of each mummy and each one held in his hand a golden cup of white sand. Set in each throne was a silver tablet in the ancient Uighur, but of such a remote period that they have not been as yet deciphered. They probably contain the names of the kings, the dates of their rule and other particulars. Around the necks of the mummies were necklaces, upon which were strung miniature models of weapons of war and domestic utensils - little golden javelins, swords, etc., and little golden pots and (missing)
(missing) utter dryness of the place, so far beneath the dry desert, had preserved all the fabrics and wood. In high chests decorated with weird designs of flowers and animals of unknown type were found pictures and writings painted upon heavy silk, and a great number of thin silver plates bearing characters in the same ancient Uighur writing.
The whole chamber, indeed, was a tremendous treasure trove of the greatest historical importance. Once the writings can be read there is little doubt that they will reveal details of a lost civilization of which only the legends of China, India and Persia speak vaguely, legends of an unknown superior race which existed in the region of the Gobi when the rest of the world was merged in barbarism and whose cities were built centuries before the Pyramids.
"The writings in the tomb," commented Dr. Lao Chin, the Chinese archaeologist associated with the Kozloff expedition, "are the books of a golden age. In the secret chambers of the old Tao temples are to be found fragments of the same kind of writing, but no one has been able to decipher them. Once a great white race inhabited what is now the Gobi. China, India and the Mediterranean countries were then inhabited only by barbarians. These men of the Gobi sent out expeditions to colonize the wilds of a savage earth. Some of them came to China and, mixing with the best of the yellow savages, became the Chinese race. Others went to Egypt, India, and Greece and northern Europe and did the same thing there. They probably even got as far as America

and were the founders of that lost civilization which was old before the Aztecs came down and found its ruined cities."

Professor Kozloff places the date of the burial of these last seven kings at between 8,000 and 6,000 B.C. The seven kings would seem to include a complete dynasty. According to the legends they ruled the whole of Mongolia and central Asia, all the Altai and Himalayan regions, and the territories now covered with a moving sand, barren of cultivation and inhabited by various nomadic tribes. The legends tell that the Gobi Desert and the highlands between the Siberian and Tibetan mountains formed at that time a cultivated land of fertile fields, forest, lakes and rivers, filled with delicious fish. Magnificently constructed highways and roads connected the various cities and towns with each other. There were well-built cities, huge temples and public institutions, elaborate private houses and palaces of the rulers.

"I could distinctly see the dried up beds of rivers, canals, and lakes and what might have been rich orchards and active life."

The first excavation under the various ruins of Khara Khoto gave evidence merely of the time of Genghis and Kubla Khans and the last days of its existence. At the time of Genghis Khan Khara Khoto was already a militaristic decadent city, greatly shrunk from its former glory. Its predominant religion of this late period was Buddhism, and its life was altogether commercial. The merchants of the West and the East came there to exchange their goods. The West brought here all its merchandise and received here gold and silver, whereas the East brought raw materials, silk and hides.

Great workshops of domestic implements and utensils of agriculture and hunting indicate that the people were not warriors or savages. Even paper money of the time of Genghis Khan was discovered in large bulks, with which the Tartar ruler paid his troops and officers. Heaps upon heaps of old Mongolian and Tartar manuscripts, pictures, garments and weapons were found in one of the burial chambers of the Black Palace and among them the first autographic documents written by Genghis Khan.

The real treasures were found far below the surface ruins, in the remains of a much more ancient city, which had preceded the other by thousands of years.

Gold was evidently the easiest and most abundant metal of the Gobi Desert, in those days. It had no more value with the ancient

Uighurs than our iron and copper. Horseshoes made of gold, appears and shovels were of silver.
Historical records say of the Uighurs that they first came to power about 7000

(break in text)
Professor Kozloff then undertook his expedition to the dead city with a special guide of Prince Tsazak.
In less than a month's journey with a caravan Kozloff's expedition arrived at the mountain range that overlooked the desolate valley with its black ruins, which at some places rose to more than fifty feet high in the air and of which he writes:
"A feeling of awe overcame us on seeing the most overwhelming ruins, perhaps the oldest metropolis of the world. All the impenetrable region. With its desolation and loneliness, lay before our eyes.

-Page break-
[apparent break in text]
Without which the venture would mean little. By presenting his friendly Mongolian Prince with a phonograph and records of the chants of lamas and songs of the shepherds, the latter became unusually friendly and said that if he could present similar marvelous objects to a number of other princes and the lamas he might get permission for the excavation of Kara Khoto.
But with the condition that he should not take away the dead, or anything that belonged to them, but see and copy everything he wished, and cover again the place with sand.
Professor Kozloff had heard frequently during his previous expeditions of the ruins of a dead city located in the province of Alashan, in the Gobi Desert, but all his efforts to secure full information of it accurate locality from the native Mongols remained fruitless. It was only through his long friendship with a Mongolian Prince, Baldyn Tsazak, near Urga, that he obtained the following allegoric decription:
"My Dear Brother - What I shall tell you is a secret that only the ruling Khans of the Gobi Desert can know. Khara Khoto - the Black City - lies aside from all the present caravan routes, over a thousand miles south of Urga, near the picturesque like of Soho Nor. The ruins are only visible to the initiated. The strangers can never see it. The phantoms of the dead are guarding its unknown

treasures. Some few bandits have tried to dig under its ruins and sell things to foreigners, but only a few have gotten away alive. Our tradition does not permit digging in the soil, and there is a penalty of death for anyone who digs up the graves of our buried ancestors."

For a long time Kozloff could not secure permission from the authorities and the inhabitants to make an expedition to Khara Khoto and start an excavation,

[break in text]

There is a good reason to believe that the various prevailing images of Buddhas, Boddhisatvas and gods and goddesses of China and India are largely copies of the ancient saints and rulers of the Uighurs as are also many of those used in the Tibetan lamaseries to-day.

[break in text]

The Uighurs, as the race was called, reached a high degree of culture: they knew astrology, mining, textile industry, architecture, mathematics, agriculture, writing and reading, medicine and Magianism. They had excellent training in decorative arts on silk, metal, and wood, and they made statues of gold and silver and wood, clay and bronze.

[break in text]

(Historical records say of the Uighurs that they first came to power about 7000) B.C. Somewhere from the south of Mongolia, from the present day province of Alashan of China, rose this white and strong nation. The origin of the Uighurs is problematic. But it is known that they ruled all the border lands of China, India and Mongolia, spread gradually northward, and eventually controlled all the more or less advanced nomadic tribes.

The greatest power of the Uighurs extended from 6000 B.C. till the rise of the new Chinese, Indian, and Persian empires. The Chinese annals of 500 B.C. describe them as being a light-haired and blue-eyed people. It was the rise of the new militant tribes, such as the Kirghiz, the Tartars of the Altai mountains, the Uriankhai and the newly formulated Mongolian races - mountaineers - that ultimately conquered the Uighurs.

Khara Khoto, as well as their other surviving old cities of Mongolia, were ultimately occupied by the hordes of Genghis Khan and Kubla Khan, and are since then buried in the sand.

About the same time as Professor Kozloff's discovery of the tombs of the Tartar kings, Professor Adrianoff excavated an ancient Uighur burial place in the Minusinsk district of Siberia, which borders on Mongolia. He found fifteen bodies mummified men on horseback, with all the equipments, buried there about 3000 B.C. On sinking a shaft down the mound he came upon a rotten beam of timber; four or five yards deeper he found mummified bodies in huge stone trunks or chests, sitting in their national garb and their faces covered with silver masks. A few yards deeper he found skulls of a dozen men and their bones in disorder. Here he found strange metallic discs of gold-bronze, the use of which is unexplainable.

A few years before Kozloff's excavation of Khara Khoto, Professor Le Coq excavated another dead city, Khotcho, in Chinese Turkestan, a thousand or more miles directly west from Khara Khoto, and discovered a vast amount of manuscripts of a latter period, mostly written in Uighur script, although the language in that case is either Persian, Chinese or Hindoo. What was the reason of those scholars or priests writing their sacred books not in Chinese or Sanskrit letters, which were at that time fully developed? The Uighur script was evidently more scholarly or appropriate to express their ideas, as the Latin was for the Gothic period, or as the Slavonic script is still used by the Russian Greek Church.

The seven buried Tartar kings seem to include a complete dynasty, covering the periods of 8000 to 7000 before our time. The astronomical charts indicate clearly the position of the constellations of that time, which closely corroborate the counting of time from the other evidence.

What new and amazing light will be shed upon the history of the world when the copies of the writings upon those strange silver plates in the tomb of the Seven Kings are at last deciphered?

A Painting of a Goddess of the Vanished Race, Photographed by Professor Kozloff in the Tomb of the Seven Kings.
A Golden Scepter of One of the Ancient Kings Found in the Secret Tomb.

"A painting of a goddess of the vanished race, photographed by Professor Kozloff in the Tomb of the Seven Kings."

"A Golden Scepter of One of the Ancient Kings Found in the Secret Tomb."

Bibliography

Part One: Historical Uighur Empire

"*Asia*". 1890. "*Asia*". Science 15 (371). American Association for the Advancement of Science: 170–75. http://www.jstor.org/stable/1764357. Downloaded 01-03-2016 from JSTOR.org

Barthold, Wilhelm; *Turkestan Down to the Mongol Invasion*; 1992

Benson, Linda; *The Ili Rebellion: The Moslem Challenge to Chinese Authority in Xinjiang 1944-1949*; 1990

Laws of Manu (The), http://www.sacred-texts.com/hin/manu.htm

Carruthers, Douglas. "*Unknown Mongolia Vol. 1*". J.B. Lippincott Company (1914). https://archive.org/details/in.ernet.dli.2015.39226/page/n9. Accessed 5-6-2016

Cleaves, Francis Woodman; *Secret History of the Mongols*; 1982

Dashtseveg, Tumen; *Anthropology of Archaeological populations from Inner Asia*; http://www.academia.edu/5976060/Anthropology_of_Archaeological_populations_from_Inner_Asia
Mongolian Journal of Anthropology, Archaeology and Ethnology, Vol. 4, № 1(312): 162-183(2008). Accessed 07-08-2016

Grousset, Rene (1997). *The Empire of the Steppes a History of Central Asia (translated by Naomi Walford)*. Rutgers University Press, New Brunswick, New Jersey

Kamberi, Dolkun
Ancient Heritage of Talklimakan & Uyghur Urbiculture; 2016
Uyghurs and Uyghur Identity; 2015

James A. Millward and Peter C. Perdue (2004). "*Chapter 2: Political and Cultural History of the Xinjiang Region through the Late Nineteenth*

Century". In S. Frederick Starr. *Xinjiang: China's Muslim Borderland.* M. E. Sharpe.

Millward, James A. (2007). *Eurasian Crossroads: A History of Xinjiang (illustrated ed.).* Columbia University Press.

Prichard, James Cowles. "*On the Ethnography of High Asia*". The Journal of the Royal Geographical Society of London 9 (1839): 192–215. Downloaded 01-03-2016 from JSTOR.org

Rossabi, Morris; *China Among Equals: The Middle Kingdom and Its Neighbors, 10th-14th Centuries*; 1983

Sinor, Denis (Ed.); *Cambridge History of Early Inner Asia*; Cambridge University Press; 1990

Soucek, Svat; *A History of Inner Asia*; 2000

E. Denison Ross and Vilhelm Thomsen; *The Orkhon Inscriptions: Being a Translation of Professor Vilhelm Thomsen's Final Danish Rendering* https://archive.org/stream/Ross1930BSOASOrkhon/Ross_1930_BSOAS_Orkhon_djvu.txt. Accessed 08-15-2016.

Part Two: Other Depictions of the Great Uighur Empire

Andrews, Shirley; *Lemuria and Atlantis Studying the Past to Survive the Future*;

Berkmen, Haluk; *The Ancient Uighur (Uygur) Empire Dr. Haluk BERKMEN*; http://tdtkb.org/content/ancient-uighur-uygur-empire-do%C3%A7-dr-haluk-berkmen; accessed 10-4-2017

Churchward, James
Lost Continent of Mu Motherland of Men; 1926
Copies of Stone Tablets Found by William Niven at Santiago Ahuizoctla Near Mexico City; 1927
Books of the Golden Age; 1927
Children of Mu; 1931
Lost Continent of Mu; 1931
Sacred Symbols of Mu; 1933

Cosmic Forces of Mu Vol. 1; 1934
Cosmic Forces of Mu Vol. 2; 1935

Cserep, Jozeph; *America as the Prehistoric Cradle of the Caucasian Race*; correspondence with James Churchward. Undated.

Hanioglu, M. Sukru; *Ataturk: An Intellectual Biography*; 2011

Spaulding, Baird T.
Life and Teaching of the Masters of the Far East Volumes 1-5

Parker, Edward Harper; *China, Her History, Diplomacy, and Commerce: From the Earliest Times to the Present Day*; 1901.

Santesson, Hans Stefan; *Understanding Mu*; 1970

Earll, Tony (Raymond Buckland); *Revealing Mu*; 1970

Sima Qian; *Records of the Grand Historian*

William of Rubruck; *The journey of William of Rubruck to the eastern parts of the world*, 1253-55 page 208, https://archive.org/stream/journeyofwilliam00ruys/journeyofwilliam00ruys_djvu.txt. accessed 09-23-2017

Index

CPSIA information can be obtained
at www.ICGtesting.com
Printed in the USA
FSHW021248030719
59695FS